k

Ron Jones

Liverpool History Press

First Published in Great Britain 2004 by Ron Jones Associates Limited.

ISBN 978-0-9573833-4-0

Written and photographed by Ron Jones.

Design: Ron Jones / Pami Deol.

Published by the Liverpool History Press.

Email: books@rja-mpl.com

Printed in China.

Acknowledgements

The author would like to thank Dr Adrian Jarvis for making numerous helpful suggestions and for proofreading the first edition. For those who wish to delve deeper into the history of Albert Dock, *Albert Dock: Trade and Technology,* edited by Dr Arian Jarvis and Kenneth Smith, Liverpool, 1999 (ISBN 0 906367 99 9), is highly recommended.

Thanks are also due to the staff of National Museums Liverpool, Tate Liverpool, The Beatles Story and Liverpool Record Office for their helpful assistance.

Nearly all of the images used in this book have been taken by the author or are from his substantial collection of historic images of Liverpool and Merseyside. A small number of images were supplied to him by the former Merseyside Development Corporation or are from the archives of the Liverpool Record Office and National Museums Liverpool.

LHP

Liverpool History Press

www.liverpoolhistorypress.co.uk

Contents

Albert Dock
Liverpool

This book tells the story of how Albert Dock was built, how it prospered for some fifty years, became obsolete and, within a relatively short time, spiralled into disuse and, finally, decay and abandonment. It also chronicles how, miraculously, it was re-born as the jewel in Liverpool's crown, supporting a vibrant community of world-class visitor attractions, hotels, shops, restaurants and bars, luxury apartments and commercial offices.

Once a blot on the landscape, Albert Dock has become symbolic of the renaissance that has been taking place in Liverpool throughout the latter part of the 20th century and into the 21st century. Indeed, Albert Dock has rightly been credited with being the catalyst for much of the new development that has taken place in the city's extensive disused docklands. Albert Dock is the region's top visitor attraction and is at the heart of Liverpool's World Heritage Site.

The process of regeneration gathered pace with Liverpool's celebration of its 800th anniversary in 2007 and its year in the spotlight as European Capital of Culture in 2008. In fact, the City's four biggest projects in decades – Liverpool One, the Liverpool Arena & Convention Centre at King's Dock, the Museum of Liverpool and the Mann Island developments – now surround Albert Dock on three sides. The photograph opposite was taken before any of these developments had begun.

Finally, to look at Albert Dock in isolation would give a blinkered view, so its story is properly set within the context of the City and Port of Liverpool and the historical period in which it was built.

ZEBU

Jesse Hartley 1780 – 1860: creator of Albert Dock

The fact that Jesse Hartley died at the age of 80 on 24th August 1860 whilst still working as 'Chief Engineer' of the Liverpool Docks, a job he had been doing for 36 years, speaks volumes about the man. As an aside, it is an interesting coincidence that Thomas Steers, Liverpool's first Dock Engineer, also worked until he was 80.

A Yorkshireman, born into an engineering family in the Yorkshire town of Pontefract on 21st December 1780, Jesse Hartley followed in his father's footsteps and trained as a stone mason. We first hear of him in 1804 working on the bridge at Ferrybridge, built by his father, Bernard Hartley, who was Surveyor of Bridges to the West Riding of Yorkshire. Between 1805 and 1808 father and son collaborated on the building of the road bridge over the River Calder at Castleford.

Hartley spent the best part of the next decade working on bridges and construction projects in Ireland, returning with his Irish bride in 1818 to take up a new job as Bridgemaster for the Salford Hundred. Six years later, with no dock construction experience, he beat thirteen other candidates to win the prized appointment of Deputy Surveyor of the Liverpool Docks. Within eight months he was promoted to 'Civil Engineer and Superintendent of the Dock Estate', in effect 'Chief Engineer' of the Port of Liverpool.

Nowadays, Hartley is known simply as 'the man who built Albert Dock'. What is not so well-known is that, in a dazzling career stretching 36 years, he masterminded the unprecedented expansion of the Liverpool docks at a time when Liverpool was the boomtown of Victorian England. He quadrupled the size of the docklands from 45 to over 210 acres and in so doing either constructed or altered every dock in the town. In the process he added 140 acres of wet docks and some ten miles of quay space.

Examples of Hartley's fanciful designs, and the superb skills of Victorian stonemasons, at the entrance to King's and Wapping Docks: left is the Hydraulic Tower, right is the Gatekeeper's Lodge. Both were built in 1856.

"... hideous pile of naked brickwork."

Sir James Picton, architect, surveyor, Liverpool's most famous historian, and a contemporary of Hartley, has left us with a graphic description of Jesse Hartley:

> "For thirty-six years he guided with a despotic sway the construction of some of the mightiest works of the kind ever erected. Personally he was a man of large build and powerful frame, rough in manner, and occasionally even rude, using expletives which the angel of mercy would not like to record: sometimes capricious and tyrannical, but occasionally, when he was attached, a firm and unswerving friend. Professionally he had grand ideas and carried them into execution with a strength, solidity and skill that have never been exceeded...For a man of his undoubted mental power he was singularly slow of speech."

Generally fulsome in his praise for Hartley the man, Picton was no admirer of Hartley the architect. In the context of Hartley's Disneyesque design for a hydraulic accumulator tower at Canada Dock, Picton said of his merits as an engineer: "... a feeling for the beautiful was certainly not one of them."

He was highly critical of Albert Dock, dismissing it as "..simply a hideous pile of naked brickwork." and...

> "The works for strength and durability are unsurpassable, but it is to be regretted that no attention whatsoever has been paid to beauty as well as strength. The enormous pile of warehouse which looms so large upon the river, and its vastness surpasses the pyramids at Cheops, is simply a hideous pile of naked brickwork. Jesse Hartley had a sovereign contempt for the beautiful, but surely among the merchant princes who interested themselves in the structure, some might have been found to advocate the mere fraction of expense which would have converted the present incarnation of ugliness into something which would have dignified the commercial by allying it with the beautiful."

Times change and very few people today would agree with Picton! Remember too that Picton was an architect commenting on the work of Hartley, an engineer, so professional jealousies may well have bubbled to the surface.

Hartley's Victoria Tower at the entrance to Salisbury Dock is still there but is in a disgraceful condition and is in urgent need of restoration by its owner, Peel Holdings.

Hartley may not have been the best of communicators – he dreaded having to appear before committees and he could be irascible – but, by God, he got things done! A man of vision, with grand ideas and the technical and practical skills to turn those ideas into reality, he strode like a Colossus through the docklands of mid-19th century Liverpool. He was also blessed with amazing energy. During his first sixteen years as Chief Engineer he even managed to find the time to act as consultant on a wide range of construction projects including Chester's Grosvenor Bridge, the Liverpool and Manchester Railway and the Manchester, Bolton and Bury Canal.

Perhaps he was stretching himself a bit too thinly for, in 1840, the Dock Trustees asked him to devote all his formidable energies to the expansion and improvement of Liverpool's docks.

Whilst Hartley built on a grand scale – and they don't come any grander than Albert Dock – no detail was too small to escape his critical eye. Something of a perfectionist as well as a workaholic, he had the sole and unquestionable power to reject out of hand any bricks that did not meet his extremely precise specification. Moreover, the rejected bricks had to be removed from the site by the contractor within 24 hours. It has been estimated that 23.5 million bricks were used in the construction of Albert Dock. No contractor with any sense would want to get on the wrong side of Jesse Hartley.

Already an 'old age pensioner', Hartley was nevertheless still in his prime and at the height of his powers in 1841 when he started to build Albert Dock. Remember too that Albert Dock was not the only thing on his mind for by that time he was heading up a 'direct works' department of 528 people with an enormous range of responsibilities throughout the whole of Liverpool's burgeoning docklands.

More than 170 years later, Albert Dock continues to dazzle us. It is as sound and as impressive today as when Hartley built it. You would be hard-pressed to come up with the name of anybody who has done as much for Liverpool as Jesse Hartley, yet you will search the city in vain for a statue of him. Perhaps 'his' Albert Dock is memorial enough.

The Royal Visit: The Prince Consort opens Albert Dock

THE ROYAL VISIT: THE PRINCE CONSORT OPENS ALBERT DOCK

As Britain's second 'Gateway to Empire', Liverpool was no stranger to the comings and goings of the great and the good from the four corners of the earth. Just ten days before Prince Albert's visit the town had welcomed the Viceroy of Egypt, Ibrahim Pasha. He proved a popular visitor and was warmly and enthusiastically welcomed by the crowds who, with typical Liverpudlian wit, immediately 're-christened' him Abraham Parker.

However, Prince Albert's visit, to open the Albert Dock and lay the foundation stone of the Sailors' Home, was in an altogether different league. This was the first 'state visit' by a member of the British royal family in the city's history. And Liverpool made sure that it was a triumph.

As an indication of its national, as well as local, importance, the August 1 edition of The Pictorial Times is largely given over to the Prince's visit to Liverpool, as the following extracts show:

> "JULY 30.– At half-past eleven this morning, his Royal Highness Prince Albert arrived from London by special train. The mayor, Mr. Laurence, the chairman of the railway company, Lord Adolphus Fitzclarence, Sir Wm. Arbuthnot, Sir Wm. Warre, and thirty-six other gentlemen were in the yard to receive him. As the train emerged from the tunnel, the band of the 30th regiment struck up "God save the Queen." On leaving the carriage he was received by the gentlemen already named, and by Earl Talbot, Lord Sandon, Mr. Booth &c. He first shook hands with the mayor and then with the noblemen and gentlemen who were presented to him. On the conclusion of the anthem, his Royal Highness stepped into his open carriage and drove off to the lodgings prepared for him. The streets were crowded to excess. Order outside the station was kept by a detachment of the 4th Light Dragoons and a strong body of police.

The best vantage points sold for up to 35 guineas. Special stands and stages were erected along the route with standing room for the public costing upwards of two shillings. Most businesses closed for the day: Liverpool virtually declared its own Bank Holiday.

"After an interval of half an hour, his Royal Highness left his lodgings in St. Anne Street, and proceeded in state along the line of streets to the town hall. His reception was most enthusiastic; balconies were erected along the line of procession, and these and the windows of the houses were filled with gay and animated parties. There was a most brilliant display of flags, banners &c. All business is suspended. There are 200,000 strangers in town, and all the inhabitants are in the streets. All is gaiety and splendour.

"Upon arrival at the Town Hall the Prince and suite alighted at the principal entrance amid the enthusiastic cheers of a dense multitude. He was received at the entrance by the mayor, recorder, town clerk, and office bearers, in their several robes of office; the members of the corporation on being drawn up in file on each side of the entrance hall, and at once proceeded up the grand staircase. We have referred to the embellishments which the noble Town Hall has recently undergone, and it has today presented the most unique appearance that can well be imagined. The head of the staircase was filled with elegant shrubs, which blended with the embellishments of the walls, statuary, &c., in a most charming manner. Upon reaching the small drawing room which was already almost filled with elegantly-dressed ladies, the address was read by the Recorder, dressed in his full robes of office, and afterwards presented to the Prince."

Prince Albert listens to the civic address being read out in the Town Hall.

Following the delivery of the address and the Prince's response – "With considerable speed his Royal Highness drove down to the docks, and went instantly on board the *Fairy*, accompanied by Bramley Moore [sic], Esq., chairman of the Dock Committee, Lord

After disembarking onto the quayside of Atlantic Pavilion, Prince Albert was introduced to Jesse Hartle and complimented him on "the great skill displayed in the construction of the stupendous docks an warehouses". Admission to Albert Dock that day was an all-ticket affair for the thousands of spectato – "the elite of the town". The reporter from the Liverpool Mercury was particularly impressed by th ladies of Liverpool: "Even overshadowed as they were by the vast stacks of warehouses, the 'fairest c the fair' looked loveliness itself. Clad in the richest garments, the 'Lancashire witches' graced th scene...Nothing could exceed it in grandeur and effect – it was a gorgeous spectacle."

Morpeth, and the naval officers of the port. The *Fairy* quickly flew across the river to the Cheshire side, and steamed along that side for about three miles, up to the lazarette ships, followed by a fleet of steamers of all sizes, to the number of forty.

"From the Cheshire side of the river the *Fairy* crossed to the Liverpool side, and returned along the line of docks amidst the cheers of assembled thousands and the roar of artillery. The sight was really magnificent, all the ships in the docks were decked out in gayest colours and the river was crowded with boats filled with people. At half-past two the *Fairy* entered the dock, where were assembled two thousand ladies and gentlemen, the elite of the town; they cheered enthusiastically, which his Royal Highness returned, and in order to gratify the crowd sailed round the dock.

Designed to store bales, hogsheads and puncheon this floor in the Atlantic Pavilion warehouse wa converted into an elegant dining room.

"At half-past three his Royal Highness entered the room, where a *dejeuner* for 1000 persons was prepared. On the Princes right sat his suite, Lord Sandon, Lord Morpeth, &c; on his left Mr Bramley Moore (the mayor) [sic], Earl Talbot, Lord Fitzclarence, W. Brown, Esq., M.P., Thomas Thornley Esq., M.P., &c. &c....

"There were eight tables from north to south, nearly 100 feet each in length, besides the top, or Court table. As on all similar "state" occasions, the viands were cold, but choice and excellent. The whole of this splendid dejeuner was provided by Mr. Lynn, of the Waterloo Hotel, and the provision and arrangements were highly creditable to that gentleman, who is perhaps one of the first providores in the provinces of England, and difficult to be surpassed, if equalled, in the metropolis itself.

"The ornaments in confectionery, &c., on the tables were most splendid, including gilded stands or piéces montés supported by quaint or classical figures; picturesque representations of rural scenery, castles, windmills on rocks; one hundred stands for pineapples alone, all of different and beautiful designs, and other ornaments.

"On each side of the chairman's seat were two large splendid solid silver ornaments."

The Town Hall's Large Ballroom, with its huge chandeliers and Minstrels' Gallery, has changed little since the Prince's visit. See also page 61.

After leaving Albert Dock, the Prince returned to the Judges' House in St Anne Street. In the evening he visited the Blue Coat School and attended a grand banquet held at the Town Hall in his honour by the mayor and council. To round off the first day of his visit, a spectacular firework display was staged at public expense.

A no-expense-spared bedroom at the Judges' House had been specially prepared for the 'illustrious sojourner'. It was done out in Louis Quatorze style using the finest materials and furniture. So much attention had been lavished on this room "for the repose of Prince Albert after the triumphs of the day..." that it was even likened to a scene from a Rembrandt painting.

At 11.00am the following day, Friday, 31 July, Prince Albert left the Judges' House for his final public engagement – the laying of the foundation stone of the Liverpool Sailors' Home in Canning Place. Again, huge crowds, as well as an official procession of nearly seven thousand people, turned out to see him.

The Sailors' Home was a magnificent building which survived the bombs of Hitler's Luftwaffe but succumbed to the pencils and slide rules of the city planners. It was closed down in 1969 and razed to the ground in the early 1970s. To this day Liverpool has a propensity to destroy its heritage in the name of 'progress'.

Prince Albert lays the first stone of the Liverpool Sailors Home with the magnificent trowel specially commissioned for the occasion. It later 'went missing' from the Royal Collection at Windsor Castle and its whereabouts are still unknown.

After returning to the Judges' House once again, the Prince finally left for Lime Street railway station at 3.40pm to catch the royal train back to London.

Prince Albert could not have failed to be impressed by the warmth and depth of the welcome he had received in Liverpool and no doubt delivered an enthusiastic report to Queen Victoria. Five years later, on the 8th and 9th October, 1851, Prince Albert, Queen Victoria, and their children came *en famille* to see for themselves 'the wonders of Liverpool', including, of course, Albert Dock.

The Albert Dock Story
Part 1: A colossus is born

THE ALBERT DOCK STORY – PART 1: BIRTH OF A COLOSSUS

Liverpool had already achieved a notable 'first' when, in 1710, Thomas Steers began construction of the world's first enclosed commercial wet dock. Opened to shipping in 1715, but not finally completed until 1720, the Old Dock as it later became known, was located where Liverpool One is today, just across the road from Albert Dock.

Liverpool's burgeoning trade, however, meant that within 20 years the Old Dock could not cope and Steers, in the meantime appointed as the town's Dock Engineer – a 'first' for Liverpool and Britain – drew up plans for another dock, Salthouse. This opened in 1753 and, spurred on by Liverpool's rapid growth as a port, was soon followed by George's Dock and King's and Queen's Docks. By the end of the 18th century, when the town's population had been propelled from 5,000 to 80,000 Liverpool was the country's second port and had the beginnings of a proper dock system under the control of one body. Indeed, Liverpool remained the country's largest single port authority until 1908 when, in a deliberate act of imitation, the Port of London Authority was formed.

It would be nice to claim that Albert Dock was the first enclosed dock with quayside warehouses but we can't since it was preceded by London's St Katharine's Dock in 1828. The power to build docks of this kind was granted by the 1803 Warehousing Act but for various reasons nothing concrete was achieved in Liverpool until the Bill to construct Albert Dock was lodged in 1841. By that time around 200 bonded warehouses had sprung up all over the town, a nightmare for HM Customs to supervise and ensure that the Government received its due revenues.

The idea behind a dock such as Albert is that goods could be loaded straight from ship to quayside bonded warehouse and checked when it was convenient to HM Customs. By these means ships could be unloaded and turned round much faster. Before Albert was built the unloading of ships in Liverpool could take up to three weeks. In London, two days would not be unusual.

The other major reason the Government was keen to see Liverpool adopting the St Katharine's Dock model is that the Liverpool system or, to be precise, lack of system, was that fraud, evasion, pilferage and, let's not mince words, downright plunder, was being undertaken on a massive scale. Amazingly, Liverpool's vested interests were able to thwart the Government for some 40 years.

When Jesse Hartley set out in 1841 to design the port's first integral dock warehousing scheme it had to accommodate the biggest ships in the world. No doubt the emergence of 1,000-ton vessels such as Isambard Kingdom Brunel's great iron steamship *Great Britain*, the largest ship of its day, was uppermost in Hartley's mind. Launched in 1843, the world's first ocean-going steamship set out from nearby Coburg Dock on her maiden voyage to New York on 26th July 1845. A short distance away the first ships were starting to use Albert Dock.

It is interesting to note that Cunard's biggest liner, the 1,132 ft long *Queen Mary 2,* weighs nearly 149,000 tonnes and carries over 2,600 passengers and 1,250 crew. By comparison, *Great Britain* was a mere 322 ft long and had room for only 252 passengers.

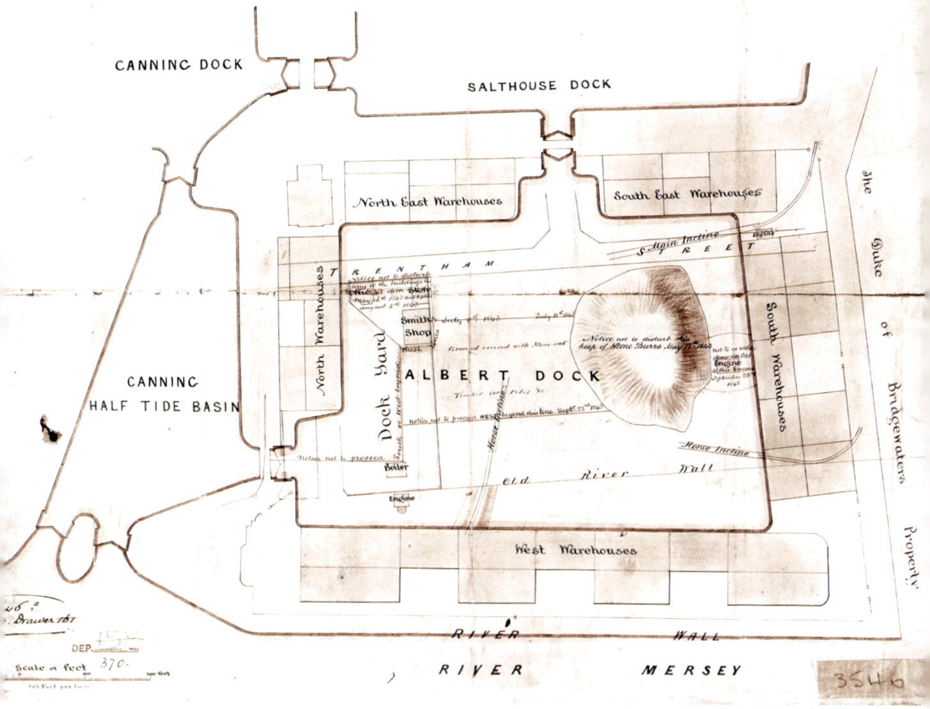

Jesse Hartley's 1843 working drawing.

The site chosen for Albert Dock was bounded to the east by Salthouse Dock and Cornhill, to the south by Duke's Dock and to the north by the river entrance to Canning Dock. Trentham Street ran through the centre of the site. Altogether, 59 occupiers, including shipbuilding and timber yards, warehouses, the Dock Trustees' own dock-yard and even some houses and an ale house, would disappear. Part of the site would have to be reclaimed from the Mersey.

The dock basin itself would have a water area of 7.75 acres. Passages would lead to the old Salthouse Dock and to a new Canning half-tide basin with a double entrance from the River Mersey. The five stacks of warehouses, each five storeys high plus basement vaults, would provide 1.25 million sq ft of storage accommodation. For added security, the dock would be encircled by a high wall; the only surviving part of this wall can be seen along the riverside promenade. The icing on the cake would take the form of a monumental river wall with a Marine Parade for the enjoyment of the public.

Material man

No less than six different designs were drawn up by Hartley at prices ranging from £33.10s to £70.14s per square yard. Each design was tested by him. For example, their fire resistance was put to the test by building a structure 18ft square by 10ft high, filling it with timber and barrels of tar and pitch and setting it on fire. The brick and cast iron structure fared better than the iron-lined wooden one which was ablaze after 45 minutes. Economy was also an important consideration: cast iron was cheaper than granite and was chosen for the columns lining the quaysides.

Albert Dock, as a structure, was built entirely of cast iron, brick, sandstone and granite. So why did Hartley place an order for thousands of beech and elm trees? So that he could drive 13,729 piles of timber, equivalent to 48 miles in length, deep into the river bed to provide the foundations for his giant stacks of warehouses, is the answer. In fact, part of Albert Dock is built on quicksand and rises and falls with every tide.

At ground level the massive load-bearing brick walls are over 3ft thick whilst at fourth floor level they are still 19 inches thick. Small wonder that some 23.5 million bricks were used...and they all had to meet the eagle-eyed Hartley's quality control process. Small wonder too that the original contractor appointed to supply bricks was unable to keep pace with demand and had to be supplemented by another contractor. Laying all these bricks took 47,000 tons of mortar.

Perhaps the dock's most striking visual feature is the monumental Greek Doric-style cast iron columns, nearly 15ft high by 12.5ft in circumference, perched on the very edge of the quay-sides. The edges of those quaysides, the retaining walls of the docks and passages and the river wall have been fashioned out of granite in Hartley's trademark Cyclopean style i.e. blocks of irregularly shaped granite dressed only on the outside face. In fact, so much granite was to be used that Hartley persuaded the Dock Committee to open its own quarry in Kirkcudbrightshire, Scotland, and build a coaster, the *Oak*, to carry the granite and timber to Liverpool. Such was the skill of Hartley's stonemasons in constructing dock walls and quaysides out of stone of all shapes and sizes, it has been suggested that they could do three-dimensional jigsaws in their sleep!

Clockwise: one of Jesse Hartley's 'trademark' cyclopean stone walls; barrel-vaulted brickwork under the quayside colonnades; cast iron portico of the Dock Traffic Office; mooring ring and keystone between two slabs of quayside granite.

Renovated section of the Colonnades vaults, now used as a residents' car park.

The five detached piles of warehouses were vaulted throughout from top to bottom with rows of massive cast iron pillars and beams to support the arches. Below ground were immense vaults which would not have looked out of place in the crypt of a Gothic cathedral, particularly the southwest corner where they are built of stone.

Also out of sight but no less impressive is another Hartley, and world, 'first' – the stressed-skin wrought iron roof designed for the warehouses, the first completely fireproof roof of its kind. Shaped for the most part like the upturned hull of a ship, the roofs were fashioned out of wrought iron plates, rivetted and galvanised, with a system of iron trusses. Liverpool was an early and enthusiastic user of cast iron materials and could boast construction of the world's first cast iron church, St George's, Everton, in 1814.

With its cast iron portico, architrave and pediment, the Dock Traffic Office has been described as a 'monument to cast iron architecture'.

Built quickly but built to last

Victorian legal processes were obviously quicker than today for, within a year, all the land acquisitions were completed. By November 1841 Hartley was on site running Salthouse and Canning Docks dry so that he could construct the passages into Albert Dock. Six months later Canning Dock was open again to shipping and Hartley was making good progress on preparing the site for Albert Dock itself and creating new dock entrances.

With the start of the contract for digging the new dock basin, hundreds of navvies toiled around the clock seven days a week. At the same time the new river wall, capable of withstanding the Mersey's raging tides of 30 plus feet, was being built. By the middle of 1844 most of the dock had been constructed and work was progressing well on the warehouse stacks. The two cast iron swing bridges between Albert and the Canning Half-Tide basin and Salthouse Dock were also in place.

By February 1845 the dock was ready to receive its first ships, albeit just for lying-up. By 30th July 1846, the day Prince Albert came to Liverpool to formally grace the dock with his name, Albert was open for business proper, although the warehouse blocks were not finally completed until the following year. The elegant dock office was added in 1848, as was a clock tower on Edward Pavilion. Various other buildings such as the four houses provided for key employees, the dockmaster's office, the cooperage and additional warehousing were added during the first half of the 1850s. In 1878 the Pump House was built as part of Albert Dock's extended hydraulic system, although it should be noted that Albert had hydraulic cargo-handling equipment from the time the dock was completed in 1847 – another world 'first'.

View of Salthouse Dock, taken in 1897 from the roof of Edward Pavilion. The corner of Atlantic Pavilion can be seen on the right. Note also the quayside transit sheds, now demolished.

This late 19th century view of Canning Half-Tide Dock shows that the Albert Dock complex was still very much of the sailing ship era. To the right is the chimney of what is now the Pumphouse pub. Behind is John Foster's masterpiece, the huge and magnificent Custom House. It would have been very familiar to Liverpudlians and visitors passing through Liverpool from the 1830s through to the 1940s. It was damaged during World War Two air raids but, despite being repairable, was demolished, one of many historic Liverpool buildings which suffered the same post-war fate. It is said, with some justification, that the City Fathers and planners finished the job that Hitler had started. Ironically, historic buildings in a number of German cities (e.g. Dresden and Frankfurt) were lovingly rebuilt after the war despite suffering far worse damage than the Custom House.

The site of the Custom House began as a muddy pool upon which was built Liverpool's, and the world's very first enclosed commercial wet dock. When this became too small for the booming port, it was filled in and replaced by the Custom House. An exceedingly ugly 1960s office block and fire station then occupied the site. Today it forms part of the Liverpool One shopping complex where a glass-covered peephole reveals part of the structure of the 'Old Dock'. Like to guess what will be here in the 22nd century?

The working dock

Albert was virtually a 'port within a port'. More than that it was Liverpool's, and arguably the world's, first fully enclosed, fireproof and theft-proof, system of dock warehouses fitted throughout with mechanical handling equipment. The hydraulic lifts supplied by William Armstrong formed the world's first hydraulic cargo handling system. In its day, Albert Dock was state-of-the-art, and then some.

Prior to Albert, cargoes would be unloaded onto open quaysides and be at the mercy of thieves, smugglers and the elements. Goods could also be damaged by repetitive handling. The cargoes at Albert would be unloaded by 'modern' appliances straight onto the open, but covered, quaysides situated between the vaults and the upper floors.

This was a system that suited the cargoes for which Albert was designed – imported, high-value goods from North and South America, the West Indies and the Far East. Albert's stock in trade for more than 50 years included rum, sugar, tea, rice, dyestuffs such as indigo and gambier, tobacco, silks, hemp and cotton: it has been estimated that the above-ground storeys could hold 234,950 bales of cotton. Other exotic imports included spices, ivory and animal horns – 27,000 horns were received at Albert Dock in three months alone during 1855.

Canning No.1 Graving Dock, pictured around the turn of the 20th century. Constructed in the 1760s, slaveships were made ready here for their lengthy voyages to the coast of West Africa, then to the West Indies or America and back again to Liverpool – the notorious 'triangular trade'. Voyages could take up to two years or longer. Fittingly (ironically?), and quite literally a stone's throw away, is the International Slavery Museum, opened in 2007. This dock was deepened by Jesse Hartley in the 1840s to accommodate larger sailing ships.

Albert Dock dominated Liverpool's East Indies trade for thirty years. By the time Albert had been operating for ten years it was earning over half of the port's Far East revenue; as an indicator of its popularity, the Dock was receiving nearly 90% of Liverpool's imports of silk from China.

By the last decade of the 19th century Albert's trans-oceanic trade had fallen away and European trade became more important, peaking at the time of Queen Victoria's death in 1901 but continuing for some time after. This trade included sugar, mixed cargoes and, something of a Liverpool institution, T & J Harrison's brandy boats – small steamers that shuttled between the Bay of Biscay and Albert Dock.

Changing patterns of trade, the ever-increasing transition from sail to steam, the access and maneuverability difficulties presented to larger ships by Albert's narrow and shallow entrances and the emergence of larger, more convenient and accessible docks at Liverpool and across the Mersey at Birkenhead, were all nails being driven into Albert's coffin. By 1920 the lid was on that coffin and Albert Dock was 'dead in the water' as a commercial dock for use by ships. Nevertheless, the warehouses continued to earn good money virtually to the end, storing goods brought in by barge and, to a lesser extent, road and rail.

In this photograph, probably taken around the turn of the 20th century, a large three-masted sailing ship takes up most of the quayside of present day Edward Pavilion. Also noticeable is the quayside transit shed and the ornate clock tower and weather-vane, both long gone. Timekeeping and wind direction were important elements of port operations in the days of sail.

Before she was bought from the Admiralty by the Liverpool & Glasgow Salvage Association, the Ranger, built in 1880, had already spent about 11 years as a Royal Navy gunboat in the East Indies. Among her notable salvage operations was the haul of over £75m (at 2010 prices) of gold and silver bullion from the wreck of the SS Oceana in 1912 and assisting with the rescue of the American-owned liner SS Minnehaha, which ran aground in the Scilly Isles in 1910. After each salvage job Ranger would return to her berth at Albert Dock. She was finally broken up in 1947 after 67 years service. *Also see P31.*

Albert at war

As the country's most important lifeline for food and supplies, Liverpool was an obvious target for the Luftwaffe. As early as July 1940, Grand Admiral Raeder, head of the German Navy, who was having great success against Allied shipping with his U-boats, was imploring Hitler to send bombers *en masse* to pound Liverpool to oblivion. He argued that the destruction of this most vital port would bring Britain to its knees and force it to pay heed to a peace offer. Happily, Hitler did not at that time respond with any real commitment.

The air raids against Liverpool had begun almost comically. The first incident, on 16th July 1940, demolished the roof of one house. Apart from giving the eight sleeping occupants a rude awakening, the only fatalities were two pet budgies. However, by November 1941, when the Luftwaffe had stopped targeting Merseyside, nearly 3,900 people had been killed and another 4,500 seriously injured.

Albert Dock was requisitioned by the Admiralty during the war so that it could play its part in the Battle of the Atlantic. It was strictly off-limits and no wartime photographs have come to light. Not surprisingly, the dock was one of the Port's many casualties; shipping had been bombed in the dock basin and extensive damage had been caused to its warehouses – over 14% of the dock's floorspace was put out of action. Nicholas Monsarrat, the famous Liverpool-born author of the 1951 best-selling Battle of the Atlantic novel *The Cruel Sea,* was based at Albert Dock on board the corvette HMS *Campanula*. At the height of the May Blitz, he described watching a land mine, tethered to a parachute, dropping into the water just twenty yards from his ship. The *Campanula* was the only corvette in the dock that night, the 3rd May 1941 – *nine* of them had been berthed there the previous day. Afraid that the motion of the engine would cause the mine to explode, the crew used muscle-power to manhandle the ship out of

This 1935 photograph of Royal Navy corvettes gives a flavour of how the dock may have looked during World War II.

harm's way. When the mine did eventually explode, it sank the Mersey Docks & Harbour Board's lightship *Sirius* and a launch and damaged one of its camels.

Albert Dock has had a long association with the Royal Navy. Part of the land upon which the dock was built was once a shipyard that built fighting ships for the navy, as well as merchantmen and, no doubt, slaveships. Royal Navy ships, and vessels from foreign navies, continue to be frequent visitors.

Pictured above in Salthouse Dock is the naval training vessel HMS Eagle. Originally a 74-gun third rate ship of the line launched in 1804, she was reduced to 50 guns in 1830 and then became a training school in 1860. She was renamed HMS Eaglet in 1918, gutted in a fire in 1926 and sold as a wreck in 1927. The ship's wheel, the only surviving relic, is on display in the land-based HMS Eaglet at East Brunswick Dock nearby.

Above left: Bomb damage to Atlantic Pavilion caused during Hitler's infamous aerial 'blitzkrieg' on Liverpool in May 1941. The Dock Board made no attempt to carry out repairs and the warehouse was left exposed to the elements for almost half a century – see also the photograph on page 35. Above right: This pre-war photograph of Atlantic Pavilion shows, to the left, the Liverpool Custom House which was gutted during the same bombing raids. Also shown is the salvage vessel Ranger which saw service in both World Wars. One of her saddest salvage jobs was HMS Thetis, the Mersey-built submarine which sank during sea trials off Anglesey in 1939 with the loss of 99 men.

HMS Albury at Albert Dock, probably during the 1930s. She was a Royal Navy Hunt-class minesweeper built under the Emergency War Programme during the Great War. She saw action during World War II and took part in the Dunkirk evacuation in 1940. She carried a complement of 73 and was armed with a 4-inch anti-aircraft gun and a smaller gun. At her top speed of 16 knots she had a range of about 1,500 miles.

The Albert Dock Story
Part 2: Survival against the odds

THE ALBERT DOCK STORY - PART 2: SURVIVAL AGAINST THE ODDS

A tale of institutional vandalism, war, political intrigue, corporate greed, incompetence, procrastination, a joint last-minute rescue by 'Tarzan' and a knight in shining armour, and a phoenix-like rise from the ashes.

It is nothing less than a miracle that Albert Dock has survived. By the end of the 19th century, the Dock, designed for sailing ships and their cargoes, was obsolete - virtually the only cargo carried by sailing ships using Liverpool was salt. No surprise then that, hardly had the old Queen Victoria been laid to rest, than consideration was being given to a plan to demolish the warehouses and merge Albert and Salthouse Docks to form a modernised 'branch' dock system able to handle cargo liners, similar to its next door neighbours the Kings and Queens Docks. It was an idea but only an idea and, thankfully, its owners, the Mersey Docks & Harbour Board, took it no further.

The Board had no programme of planned maintenance for Albert Dock and the philosophy seemed to have been one of, at best, "we won't fix it til it's broken" and, at worst, "even if it is broken we still won't fix it." Nevertheless, the old dock plodded along, surviving as a storage warehouse and a 'laying-up', as opposed to a 'proper' cargo dock.

As a naval base during the Second World War, Albert Dock was an obvious target for Hitler's Luftwaffe and it did indeed take a clobbering, no more so than when a bomb blew away the north west corner of Atlantic Pavilion. By the time the May blitz of 1941 was over, more than 14% of Albert's floorspace had been put out of action.

Looking at Atlantic Pavilion today you would not know that this bomb damage was left unrepaired and the building left to the mercy of the elements for 45 years, testament both to the strength and quality of Jesse Hartley's work and the skill of the restoration team.

After the War, Albert continued its slide into terminal decline with the Dock Board, for example, deciding not to repair the worst of the bomb damage. Nevertheless, its architectural and historical importance was recognised in 1952 when it was given Grade 1 Listed Building status and again in 1976 when Liverpool City Council made it a Conservation Area.

By the mid-1960s, the hapless and cash-strapped Mersey Docks & Harbour Board could see no future for Albert Dock and wanted to get rid of it. It entered into negotiations with property developer Harry Hyams' company, Oldham Estates, to develop a 53-acre 'mini-city' of office blocks, an hotel, marina, maritime museum, restaurants and bars etc. 'Grandiose' would have been too modest a term to describe it. There were even to be direct air and river links to Liverpool Airport, a mere six miles away. The office element alone would have been eight times the square footage of the Albert warehouses. Fifty thousand jobs were to be created. In the process, the Albert warehouses were to be swept away.

Even though the Dock Board had agreed the sale of the site to Oldham Estates for £4.3m at the end of 1966, the scheme ping-ponged between the developers and Liverpool City Council, as Planning Authority for the area, for another four years. The end result was *Aquarius City*, a scaled-down, but still mammoth, scheme. No sooner had this been announced than the Dock Board's finances reached crisis point. To add to their woes, Oldham Estates decided to call it a day, pocketed their deposit and were never seen or heard from again. Albert was safe...or was it?

Abandoned and derelict

By then, as 1970 drew to a close, the Dock Board had decided to shut down the whole of the South Docks and sell off the land, although by mid-Summer everything had already been cleared from Albert's warehouses. Two years later, in September 1972, an act of great significance took place: the South Docks were finally closed, the entrance gates to the southern-most Brunswick Dock were thrown open, permanently; the entire dock system became tidal and huge quantities of sewage-polluted silt swept in from the river with every tide. In those days, if you were unlucky enough to fall into one of the docks you would more likely die of chemical poisoning than by drowning.

Redevelopment schemes galore

Whilst on Merseyside the early 70s were years of doom and gloom, nationally, the property market was booming. There was money to be made and soon the property developers were sniffing around again. The Heron Corporation wanted to build an office block on Canning Dock for re-located civil servants - the re-location of Government offices to 'depressed' areas such as Merseyside and the North East was the new 'in thing' - and offered the Board £16m for the entire South Docks. Also in the frame was Global Participants (Eire) Ltd who topped Heron's offer by £6.5m. Even Liverpool City Council had their eye on the land. They came up with a really imaginative proposal. They would seek an 85% derelict land grant from the Government and use the docks for 'landfill', in other words, as a rubbish tip!

The Dock Board was not impressed. The Council's scheme would have neutralised the land for decades. Besides, its own plan to prepare the land for development by filling in the docks with sand pumped from the River Mersey would have given it a much greater financial return than selling it to the Council at a 'derelict site' valuation.

And then there were the well-meaning but no-hope schemes. Local sculptor Arthur Dooley's was one. Arthur was one of Liverpool's most colourful characters and a scourge of the local planners; he once actually applied for the job of City Planning Officer! He set up the South Docks Development Company to develop the 300-acre site for mixed use, commissioned a feasibility study, and then? Nothing. Which is just as well for he planned to demolish the Albert warehouses and build a housing estate on the site.

Another scheme that was taken more seriously at the time was one to create a new home for Liverpool Polytechnic, now the Liverpool John Moores University. Then, as now, it was housed in different buildings spread throughout the city. The Government had even pledged £3m towards the first phase. After five years of the inertia and toytown politics that marked much of Liverpool's political scene in the 1970s, the scheme was finally aborted in 1976 after an exasperated Tory Government withdrew its offer.

Two other noteworthy schemes were being given serious consideration at around that time. One was by Pavilion Recreation Ltd., for a leisure and retail development on Wapping and Queens Docks, centred on a Tesco superstore. The other, by the mysterious Gerald Zisman who ran his business from a suburban semi, was for Albert Dock to be filled in and the warehouses demolished. Taking their place would be a World Trade Centre and office block.

Significantly, in 1974, the new Merseyside County Council was created. The rejuvenation of Liverpool's derelict docklands was placed at the top of its agenda. After years of negotiation with the Dock Company, terms were finally agreed in August 1979 for the County Council to take over the South Docks. The transfer of the first piece of land, for the County Council's new Maritime Museum, took place soon after. Now things were beginning to shape up...or were they?

Curiously, the Dock Company was still holding negotiations with Zisman and Pavilion, as well as two new developers who had entered the frame - St Katharine's Developments Ltd., whose scheme revolved around a £170m plus, 3,000-berth marina, and a £400m plus scheme by Richard Seifert and Partners, architects of London's Centrepoint and Natwest Tower, for the construction of the world's tallest building, some 600 feet taller than the Empire State Building. 'Dead in the water' and 'Pie in the sky' are phrases which would, respectively, seem to sum up these two schemes. To add to the confusion, Liverpool City Council, still the planning authority for the South Docks, disliked Merseyside County Council and was being uncooperative, if not downright obstructive.

Tarzan to the rescue

It was all becoming very messy and, a decade and a half after the Dock Board had decided to rid itself of the South Docks, still not one brick had been laid on top of another. And then, along came 'Tarzan', otherwise known as Michael, now Lord, Heseltine (pictured left). Nicknamed Tarzan because of his flowing blond hair, Michael Heseltine was the charismatic Secretary of State for the Environment in Margaret Thatcher's Government. In the aftermath of the city's Toxteth riots he had been given additional special responsibility for Merseyside. Henceforth, he was known as 'The Minister for Merseyside'. On the 14th September 1979 he announced the setting up a new quango, the Merseyside Development Corporation (MDC), which would own and rejuvenate the redundant South Docks and other derelict areas nearby, 865 acres in all. Importantly, it was to be its own planning authority. With one stroke of the pen, the warring local authorities and the ineffective Dock Company, had been sidelined.

Michael Heseltine pictured on board the 'Royal Iris' ferryboat during a Press trip to see Liverpool's derelict South Docks and the site for the International Garden Festival.

The MDC came into being in March 1981 and by August had produced its initial strategy. Taxpayers money would be used for 'pump-priming' to create confidence in the area and attract private developers. High on its list of 'must do soon' projects was the restoration of the water regime in the South Docks; water was only visible in the dock basins at high tide and there was over 40 feet of noxious sludge in places. Old and worn-out buildings were to be refurbished or removed - there were some 200 of them and half had to go - and there was much environmental landscaping to be done. Specifically, two projects stand out from those early days. One was the transformation of a former refuse tip at Otterspool into the site for the International Garden Festival which took place in the Summer of 1984 and was a runaway success. The other was Albert Dock.

Merseyside County Council had already staked its claim in the area with the first phase of its maritime museum, opened in 1980 and centred on the former Pilotage Building and the historic Canning graving docks, and was keen to expand into the Albert warehouses.The Tate Gallery, London, had put Liverpool on its short-list for a prestigious new regional gallery to house part of its national collection of modern art. And the London-based property developers, Arrowcroft, encouraged by Michael Heseltine, were taking a keen interest in Albert Dock.

Even in its totally derelict state Albert Dock was a wonder to behold, as this writer can testify. It might have oozed mud but it also oozed atmosphere. Walking through the abandoned quaysides and warehouses, inhabited only by pigeons, Arrowcroft's Chairman, the late Leonard Eppel CBE., recalls that the buildings "talked to him". He was hooked and persuaded his Board to agree to a mixed development of shops, offices and luxury apartments. Talks between MDC and Arrowcroft began in 1982 and by September 1983 they had signed an agreement. The final piece of the jigsaw, the essential *guaranteed* private sector involvement, missing from every previous scheme, was at last in place.

A phoenix in ascendance

For most of the 20th century Albert Dock had been allowed to fall into a state of gentle decay and abandonment. And then, whoosh! Within the space of a few short years the re-birth of Albert was underway... and at a break-neck speed. The race was on to complete the initial works in time for the arrival in the River Mersey of the Cutty Sark Tall Ships Race and to coincide with that Summer's International Garden Festival. It was a once-in-a-lifetime chance for Liverpool to show the world what it could achieve.

One of MDC's first priorities was the restoration of the dock system. This it did between December 1982 and August 1984. The river entrance gates at Canning island were replaced, as were the passage gates between the Canning Half-tide and Albert Docks. Docks were dredged and twelve feet of silt removed, dock walls were stabilised and repaired, the historic Hartley and Rennie Bridges were restored and two new bridges and a slipway into Salthouse Dock were built.

The Albert warehouses were in much better shape. The MDC's detailed survey had shown that generally they were in a very sound structural state. Minimal repointing of brickwork was needed. This was good news for 23.5 million bricks were used in its construction and, a century and a half later, the mortar was still rock-hard; it would have been a nightmare to repoint. In effect, Jesse Hartley built the Albert warehouses on top of a forest: the timbers from thousands of beech and elm trees were pile-driven into the Mersey mud to form the foundations for the warehouse stacks. Again, the survey found that these were in extremely sound condition. The same was true of the cast iron columns and other ironwork. All had stood the test of time. Jesse Hartley, visionary and master builder, take a bow!

As soon as the ink on its agreement with the MDC was dry, Arrowcroft was on site. The first phase of its plan was to manage the structural restoration of the Dock Traffic Office and warehouses to MDC's specification. This work was to be paid for by MDC. With its own money Arrowcroft would then fit out the quayside and mezzanine levels of Atlantic, Britannia and Edward Pavilions and its part of the Colonnades for shops and offices, respectively. This work was set for completion by early Summer 1988. The full, phased, programme of works would actually take some twenty years to complete.

Dock Traffic Office: From this...

to this...

to this.

As parts of the buildings became ready for letting, Arrowcroft would pass them to MDC (they still held the freehold in the whole of Albert Dock) and then lease them back from the MDC. Arrowcroft would also act as Estate Managers.

A dock re-born

Edward Pavilion was the first to be tackled, and with good reason. It was next door to the Maritime Museum, already under construction by Merseyside County Council which was committed to opening parts of the quaysides and a temporary exhibition in time to welcome the International Tall Ships Race in August 1984. Such was demand, the first 40 retail and office units were soon let by Arrowcroft.

August 1984: The Cutty Sark Tall Ships Races. The general public, in their thousands, were allowed access to Albert Dock's quaysides for the first time since the dock was opened by Prince Albert 138 years earlier.

It was a golden Summer for Merseyside, and the MDC. Over a four-day period, one million people flocked to see the tall ships, 160,000 of whom came to Albert Dock, curious to see the new shops, Maritime Museum exhibition and sailing ships lined up along the quaysides. For the first time since Prince Albert opened the Dock, local people and visitors from all over the world were able to have access to it. A few miles south, the International Garden Festival proved another roaring success, pulling in 3.4 million paying visitors. Confidence in Albert and the South Docks, was high and the MDC was encouraged to adopt a tourism-led strategy for its future work.

Described as a 'monument to cast iron architecture', structural restoration of the neo-classical Dock Traffic Office, including a temporary roof, was completed by Arrowcroft in October 1984. The building was then leased to Granada Television who fitted it out as a television news-gathering studio and added a new roof.

Encouraged by its success with Edward Pavilion, Arrowcroft next tackled Britannia Pavilion, sticking to its tried and tested formula of shops on the ground floor and offices on the mezzanine level. The first shops came on stream in July 1985 and these too were soon let.

Structural work on Atlantic Pavilion, which took a direct hit during a Second World War bombing raid on Liverpool's docks, began in June 1985 and was completed in June 1986. As with Edward Pavilion, the ground floor shop units and mezzanine offices were quickly let by Arrowcroft.

Urban cool. Apartment in the Colonnades, home to stars of stage, screen and football field...as well as people from all other walks of life.

Later that year the structural restoration of the biggest stack of warehouses, the Colonnades, began. The ground floor shops and first 37 apartments were ready by 1988, coinciding with the opening of the first phase of Tate Liverpool. The apartments were put on the market for between £40,000 and £80,000 and immediately snapped up. One observer described it as – "Like Sale Day at Harrods". Those early buyers were unwittingly pioneering a new, and still popular, Liverpool trend – city living.

All 115 apartments have been sold on a 150-year lease beginning on the 1st October 1985. Buyers were also able to purchase a parking space in the vaults of the Colonnades. It is interesting to ponder what the reaction would be from those old-time dockers who toiled on the top floor of Albert to the fact it now houses luxurious penthouse apartments and that Albert's warehouses have been transformed into an 'urban village', where children have been born and raised.

The decision taken in March 1985 to locate Tate Liverpool, dubbed the 'Tate of the North', in the Colonnades brought enormous kudos to Albert Dock and, of course, Liverpool. Appropriately, the Trustees chose as their architect Sir James Stirling (1926-1992), a graduate of the University of Liverpool School of Architecture and senior partner in the firm James Stirling Michael Wilford Associates.

Tate Liverpool has forced many people to look at the city in a new, more positive, light. Visitors often travel great distances to see its special exhibitions of major artists.

The first phase of Tate Liverpool, and indeed the refurbished Albert Dock itself, was officially opened in May 1988 by Prince Charles (pictured below). The gallery was an immediate success and by the time its £7 million extension opened exactly ten years later, it had easily surpassed its targets by attracting a total of over five million visitors.

Since then, numerous new developments, large and small, have taken place. The Beatles Story exhibition opened in 1990, almost doubled in size in 2008, and continues to be a major draw for fans of the Fab Four. This has been joined by two budget hotels with a total of 321 bedrooms, which are able to offer their guests unsurpassed views across the dock to the Pier Head and city centre. Large undeveloped areas of Atlantic and Edward Pavilions have been transformed into offices for large companies and the number of apartments in the Colonnades has increased to over one hundred. The bringing into use of the final undeveloped space at Albert took place in 2003 with the opening of the Premier Lodge hotel in Britannia Pavilion.

Inevitably, there have been disappointments as well as successes. Apart from sporadic events such as the Mersey River Festival and Clipper and Tall Ships Races, the dock basin continues to be a massive, under-used resource, although a link via the Pier Head from the Leeds & Liverpool Canal now attracts more visits by narrowboats to Salthouse Dock (pictured right). After an initial flourish during the first decade or so of its renaissance, the diminished retailing element at Albert Dock has also been a disappointment.

The original cost of constructing Albert, including land acquisition, was estimated at £782,265. Its present value far exceeds £230 million. More important, Albert Dock stands today as the largest, group of Grade 1 Listed Buildings in Britain. It is by far the grandest and most complete surviving example of the fully integrated Victorian warehouse dock system.

THE Joker
GOTHAM CITY

An original dockside crane on the quayside of Edward Pavilion

Then...and now

Warehouses – then, West stack, now the Colonnades and Tate Liverpool.

Atlantic Pavilion showing (left) bomb damage to North West corner.

Dock basin showing North and North East stacks, now Merseyside Maritime Museum and Edward Pavilio

Albert Dock and Canning Dock from Wapping.

South warehouse stack, now Britannia Pavilion.

Left: Undeveloped warehouse floor, Britannia Pavilion. Right: office space, Edward Pavilion.

Water quality is now up to European bathing standards and supports an abundance of marine life.

There were once four Dock/Piermaster's houses here. This is the sole survivor of World War II air raids.

Dock Traffic Office.

North warehouse stack, now Merseyside Maritime Museum.

North East warehouse stack, now Edward Pavilion.

Basement vaults, now residents' car park.

Canning Half-Tide Dock, Pump House and North Warehouse stack, now Pumphouse pub and Merseyside Maritime Museum.

A year in the life...

Albert Dock warehouses, former Dock Traffic Office and Pumphouse pub photographed from Canning Dock.

1824	Jesse Hartley appointed Dock Surveyor (Chief Engineer) of the Port of Liverpool at the age of 44. He died, still in post, when he was 80.
1841	Bill to authorise the construction of Albert Dock submitted to Parliament - Dock Act passed. Hartley authorised to give all the occupiers of the proposed site of Albert Dock notice to quit.
1841, November	Work begins on construction of Albert Dock – Canning and Salthouse Docks drained so new passages could be constructed for Albert Dock.
1842, May	Canning Dock re-opened to shipping. Good progress on site clearance and creation of new dock entrances.
1843, January	John Waring awarded contract for excavating the new dock. Apart from a few hours break at the beginning of each week, work was carried out 'round the clock'.
1845, February	First shipping, for lying-up only, allowed into the dock.
1846, 30 July	Formal opening by Prince Albert. East stacks (Edward and Atlantic Pavilions) and South East stack (Britannia Pavilion-part) opened and dock open for general shipping.
1847	Remaining warehouse stacks completed. Dock Traffic Office completed.
1848	Hydraulic warehouse hoists installed (a world first) and clock tower (designed by Phillip Hardwick) added to roof of North East stack (Edward Pavilion).
1852	Dock Master's, Assistant Dock Master's and Warehouse Superintendent's houses completed.
1853-54	West and East ends of the South stack of warehouses (Britannia Pavilion) built to meet demand for more accommodation.
1860, 24 August	Death of Jesse Hartley at the age of 80 after 36 years as Dock Surveyor.

1878	The Pump House was built as part of Albert Dock's extended hydraulic system.
1882	The majority of quayside cranes converted to hydraulic use.
1895	First, small-scale, installation of electric lighting.
1899	Part of the North stack (Maritime Museum) converted for use by the Riverside Cold Storage and Ice Company as a cold store and ice-making plant. In use until the early 1950s.
1904	Hydraulic tobacco press, formerly in use at the nearby Kings Dock tobacco warehouse, installed.
1915-16	Electric lighting installed throughout the dock.
1920	From this year, virtually no further commercial *shipping* activity in Albert Dock. However, the *warehouses* remained highly profitable into the 1960s, storing goods transported by road, rail and barge.
1939-1945	Albert Dock, along with some warehouse space, are 'requisitioned' by the Admiralty as a base for hundreds of its ships, including small warships, submarines, landing craft and merchant ships. Numerically, at no time in its history have so many ships berthed at Albert Dock. However, almost all of them were small, under 300 tons.
1940	German bomber drops a parachute mine causing damage to shipping in the dock. Later that year the Luftwaffe drops an incendiary bomb on the roof of Atlantic Pavilion.
1941, May	Extensive damage to warehouses, particularly Atlantic Pavilion, caused by Luftwaffe bombing raids during 'May blitz'. Albert 'lost' over 14% of its floor space.
1948-50	Electric lifts installed.
1952	Albert Dock given Grade 1 Listed Building status.
1960	The Mersey Docks & Harbour Board considers the demolition of Albert Dock.

1966 Negotiations begin with Oldham Estates (Harry Hyams) for the sale of Albert, Canning and Salthouse docks for a 53-acre 'mini city'. The intention was to demolish Albert Dock.

1970 Oldham Estates' revised *Aquarius City* scheme, which incorporated a 44-storey office block, announced. However, by the end of that year, by which time the Mersey Docks and Harbour Board was in financial crisis, the scheme collapsed and, in 1971, so did the Board.

1972 The entire redundant South Docks, including Albert Dock, was closed, the Brunswick dock gates were left open, the whole docks system became tidal and the silting-up process began with a vengeance.

1972-74 A variety of public and private sector schemes is proposed for Albert Dock. None of them come to pass.

1974, April Merseyside County Council comes into being. It declares that the redevelopment of the South Docks are top of its agenda and begins lengthy negotiations with the Dock Board.

1976 Liverpool City Council includes Albert Dock in a Conservation Area.

1979 Outline agreement signed by the County Council and the Dock Company on 31 August. Days later the Government announces that it is to set up a Development Corporation which will own and redevelop the South Docks.

1980	Merseyside County Council opens the first phase of the Merseyside Maritime Museum around the Canning Dock area, adjacent to Albert Dock.
1981, March	Merseyside Development Corporation set up.
1982	Agreement reached between Merseyside Development Corporation and Arrowcroft Group plc for the redevelopment of Albert Dock and plans are drawn up.
1983	Work commences.
1984	First phase opened in time for the arrival of the Tall Ships Race and International Garden Festival.
1988, 24 May	Official re-opening ceremony for Albert Dock and the new Tate Liverpool by Prince Charles, The Prince of Wales.
1990	The Beatles Story 'museum' opened.
1992	First phase of Tate Liverpool completed.
1996	Albert Dock celebrates its 150th anniversary.
1998	Second phase of Tate Liverpool completed.
2002	Final phase of undeveloped space completed.
2004	Liverpool Maritime Mercantile City, which includes Albert Dock as a key element, is inscribed as a UNESCO World Heritage Site.
2009	Canal link between Albert Dock and the Leeds & Liverpool Canal completed.

This fairly recent view of Albert Dock and the 'Three Graces' at the Pier Head, now falls into the category of 'historical'. For this classical view has been ruined by the arrival of the Mann Island development, three monolithic glass buildings (the 'Three Abominations'?), nominated for 'Building Design' magazine's 2012 'Carbuncle Cup' prize. See also page 45.

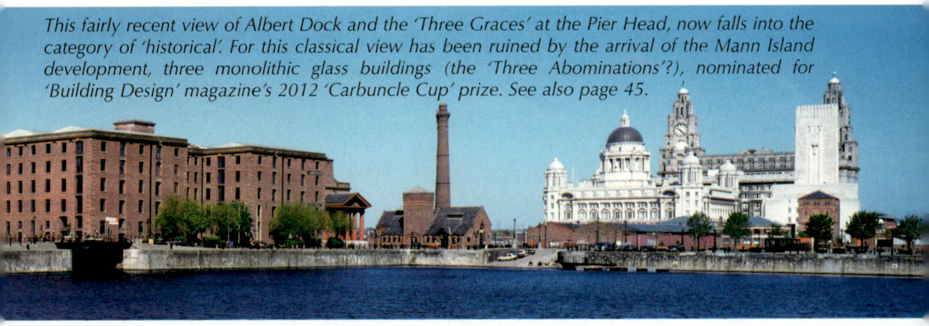

Centre: 'new kid on the block'. The Museum of Liverpool opened on 19th July 2011 at a cost of £72million – almost as much as Cristiano Ronaldo's transfer fee when he left Manchester United for Real Madrid in 2009. The museum is the largest newly-built museum in the UK for over 100 years. Architecturally, it has come in for much criticism located as it is at the heart of the city's World Heritage Site and with such illustrious neighbours as the Pier Head and Albert Dock. The museum authorities also fell out with their Copenhagen-based architects 3XN and took out a near-£4million lawsuit against replacement architects AEW for alleged defects in the building. In 2011 the museum was shortlisted for the 'Carbuncle Cup' award run annually by 'Building Design' magazine.

BROCKLEBANK

Liverpool 1846

The Royal Institution (porticoed building on left) was opened in 1817 to promote literature, science and the arts in the town. Formerly, it was the home of Liverpool merchant Thomas Parr, reputed to have the best looking house (and wife!) in Liverpool. An art gallery was opened next door in 1843.

The Prince comes to town

As Prince Albert sat down to a sumptuous banquet at Liverpool's beautiful Georgian Town Hall the evening before he formally opened Albert Dock, he would have been impressed by the view from any of its sparkling windows. The Town Hall itself had been rebuilt on a much grander scale following a disastrous fire in 1795 and no expense had been spared in fitting it out.

His hosts, the merchant princes and the great and the good of the town, had been coached in from their commodious houses in Rodney Street and the town's elegant Georgian squares or from their country mansions at Toxteth and atop the green hills of Everton.

The surrounding streets - Water Street, Dale Street, Castle Street etc., - were newly laid out in wide and handsome fashion and were already graced with fine buildings. The Tower of Liverpool with its subterranean dungeons, the last survivor of the old medieval town, had finally been swept away so that Water Street could be widened.

At the rear of the Town Hall was a spacious Exchange where the town's top-hatted and frock-coated merchants conducted their business in the open air under the gaze of a splendid public memorial to England's greatest naval hero, Admiral Lord Nelson.

Earlier that day the Prince had arrived by special train from London. The first thing he saw when he emerged from Lime Street station was Liverpool's greatest building, St George's Hall, under construction on the site of the old infirmary. The Prince took special notice of this project for, eight years earlier, its foundation stone was laid to mark the coronation of his wife, Queen Victoria. Only a town like Liverpool, bursting with Victorian pride and confidence, would have entrusted its most prestigious venture to a 'mere boy', the 23-year old architect Harvey Lonsdale Elmes. By the time it was completed in 1854, Elmes was dead, burnt out by the enormity of the task confronting him.

As he proceeded in state from his lodgings in nearby St. Anne Street to the Town Hall, the Prince would have remarked on the streets bedecked with flags and banners and crowded to excess, for the town's population was nudging towards the 350,000 mark, up from a start-of-the-century count of 80,000. Most of the townspeople were on the streets that day hoping to catch a glimpse of the noble Prince and they had been joined by another 200,000 out-of-town visitors. Amidst the euphoric cheering and flag-waving, Prince Albert may not have noticed that many amongst the jostling crowds were dirty, ragged and barefoot.

The Large Ballroom at Liverpool Town Hall, looking much the same as it did when Prince Albert was guest of honour during his 1846 visit.

Gateway to Empire

The following day the Prince would be taken down to the docks to be piped aboard the royal yacht for the start of his day of official duties. On the way, the handsome domed and porticoed Custom House, built 20 years previously and befitting a city who's port was the second most important in the entire British Empire, would have been pointed out to him. Liverpool's ships traded with virtually every country in the world, as witnessed by the proverbial 'forest of masts' of the scores of sailing ships at berth in the docks that stretched for miles along the banks of the River Mersey. Eventually, his eyes would have been drawn to the giant stacks of dock warehouses which that day would be named in his honour.

His escorts would have taken the opportunity to impress him with details of the splendid developments that had been taking place in the fields of medical and social care, education, law and order, the arts and sciences and, of course, Liverpool's lifeblood – trade and commerce. They would have told him of the town's intellectual awakening and their plans for a public library, museum and art gallery. Small wonder that the Prince, dazzled by what he had seen and heard, loftily declared: "I have heard of the greatness of Liverpool but the reality far surpasses the expectation."

The Custom House which stood opposite Albert Dock from 1839 until 1948.

The other Liverpool

But Liverpool was then, and is now, a place of violent contrast and contradiction. There was another Liverpool, one which was hidden from the Prince that day.

Liverpool then was the most densely populated and unhealthiest town in England. Dr William Henry Duncan, a lecturer at the Liverpool Royal Infirmary School of Medicine, in a shocking report three years earlier, had painted a picture of squalor, disease, misery and vice on a scale unimaginable today. People lived, no existed, at a density of 100,000 to the square mile in four types of dwelling - courts, cellars, lodging houses and 'front' houses, terraces whose houses fronted the street. Overcrowding was the norm. People lived at the rate of nearly seven to each dwelling, although in some streets over thirteen were crammed into each house. The concepts of town planning and beautification were strangers to the mean streets of Liverpool.

The 'courts' usually consisted of between six and twelve three-story houses clustered around a courtyard built on infill land at the rear of a street of terraced houses. Ventilation and lighting were poor and there were virtually no sewage facilities; only the streets where the well-to-do lived were blessed with sewers.

They did not even have an outside lavatory, a standard feature of later Victorian working class housing. Instead, residents had to use the privies and cesspits at the rear of the courts. These were little more than holes in the ground above which a simple wooden structure would offer scant privacy. They were emptied infrequently, sometimes only once a year, and they stank to high heaven.

Dr Duncan recalled visiting one small court where he noted: "...the smell arising from the uncovered ash-pits and ruinous privies and the filthy state of the court was such, that an Irishman, one of the inhabitants, said the smell was bad enough to raise the roof off his skull as he lay in bed, that was the expression he used; in that case the court was never free from disease."

Cellar dwellers

The 86,000 court dwellers, however, lived like kings compared with the 38,000 poor souls for whom 'home' was an underground cellar. Liverpool's exploding population was glad to find accommodation anywhere, even if it was a dank, airless, windowless, unpaved cellar, intended only for storage. These reeking cellars, whose floors were often covered with filthy straw, were frequently flooded by the rainwater and raw sewage which swilled down from the street above. The dirt-poor cellar dwellers quite literally did not have a pot to pee in nor a window to throw it out of.

Dr Duncan again: "...there was one cellar in Preston Street where about 30 individuals used to sleep every night; in the centre of the cellar in which they were living there was a hole dug, which was used as a receptacle for all kinds of filth; fever broke out there, and six or eight died out of the number, and those who were ill of the fever were those lying close by the side of those who had died; there was one dead man lying there at the time." Not surprisingly, outbreaks of cholera were a feature of Liverpool in the 1840s.

Swamped by the Irish

The lodging houses - simple terraced houses more often than not - were not much better. Sanitation was just as bad as in the courts but, at two-pence or three-pence a night, they did meet a need. At any one time there were some 11,000 sailors in the port and they tended to head for the lodging houses near the docks. On top of that transient population there were emigrants from every corner of Europe en route to America and the Irish, in flight from the potato famine. In the period leading up to the Prince's visit, the Irish were pouring into Liverpool at the rate of 30,000 each month. In the twelve-month period from July 1847 300,000 came.

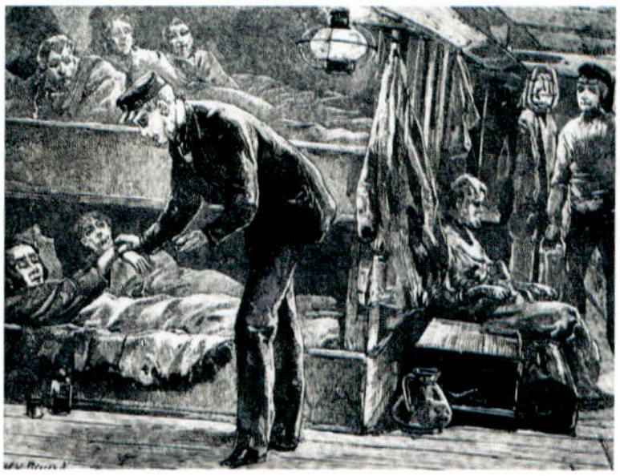

Starving, penniless and desperate, they completely overwhelmed Liverpool causing so much turbulence that 20,000 townspeople were sworn in as special constables and 2,000 troops were camped on the edge of town. The majority emigrated to America but large numbers of those who were too poor or sick to travel were left behind in Liverpool, creating their own Irish 'ghettoes' and aggravating the already dire problem of poverty. One person who was sworn in as a special constable, albeit for only one night to see at first hand how 'landsharks' preyed on unwary sailors, was the author Charles Dickens. A frequent visitor to Liverpool he always took the opportunity to roam about the docks gathering material for his books, in particular *The Uncommercial Traveller* with its graphic descriptions of the "vile haunts of vice and drink that lay in wait for poor sailors."

Long before Liverpool was swamped by the Irish in 1846 and 1847, Dr Duncan, not a man to pull his punches, was already blaming them for much of the fever in the town: "It is they who inhabit the filthiest and worst ventilated courts and cellars, who congregate the most numerously in dirty lodging houses, who are the least cleanly in their habits, and the most apathetic about everything that befalls them...By their example and intercourse with others they are rapidly lowering the standard of comfort among their English neighbours, communicating their own vicious and apathetic habits, and fast extinguishing all sense of moral dignity, independence and self-respect...I am persuaded that so long as the native inhabitants are exposed to the inroads of numerous hordes of uneducated Irish, spreading physical and moral contamination around them, it will be in vain to expect that any sanitary code can cause fever to disappear from Liverpool."

Drunk for a penny, blind drunk for twopence

Lawlessness was rife. Matters had improved somewhat after the Municipal Reform Act of 1835. At that time there were 1,200 known juvenile thieves and 3,600 prostitutes. After that date the police force had been doubled and, for the first time, they had a remit not just to lock up criminals but to *prevent* crime and vice. A few decades earlier each constable had to keep an eye on about 5,000 citizens.

Hand in glove with crime was drink, a favourite resort of the working classes, if only to escape from the hopelessness of their miserable everyday existence. Besides the ale from dozens of local breweries, cheap rum was imported by the shipload from the West Indies. At around the turn of the century every seventh house in the town was open for the sale of liquor. The 1841 census, listed 2,272 drinking places, an average of one for every 140 inhabitants. In those days you could get drunk for a penny and blind drunk for two-pence.

Short, brutalised lives

The working classes of the Liverpool of 1846 had the odds stacked against them. The principal source of work was to do with Liverpool as a port, in other words the handling of goods between ship, warehouse and railway. That work was unskilled, poorly paid and only available on a casual basis. It was degrading and insecure and produced social problems on a scale perhaps not found in any other English town. The so-called 'lower orders' were often ragged and barefoot, stunted and brutalised. They lived their wretched lives in filthy, disease-ridden hovels. The only escape from this hell on earth was death. On average, the lower classes were dead by the age of 15, although it should be borne in mind that the shockingly high infant mortality rates skewed the averages; if you made it to five your life expectancy was not too bad. Just as shocking was the complete indifference of the well-to-do citizenry to the plight of the poor, even though the poor had helped them acquire their own wealth. As might be expected, their survival rates were better. Death rate averages showed that the Grim Reaper did not come knocking on their door until they were 35.

Liverpool was the port and the port was Liverpool. The pursuit of money was the main pre-occupation of its inhabitants, causing one sharp-tongued observer to remark: "...commerce alone appears to engage the attention of the inhabitants." Leisure pursuits were scant. Apart from getting drunk, there was little else for the lower orders to do apart from watching dog fights, cock fights and bull-baiting. There were no public parks. The middle class had its bowling greens, archery and dog racing and, above all, the 'pleasures of the table' – a goodly proportion of the civic budget was blown on lavish Town Hall banquets.

Liverpool acquires a social conscience

But in the Liverpool of the 1830s and 40s change was in the air. Prior to the Municipal Reform Act of 1835, it has been claimed that the Town Council was little more than a private club which principally served the elitist interests of the town's freemen. Bribery and corruption were the norm. The other inhabitants of the town were left largely to fend for themselves.

Conditions were so bad in the town that, out of sheer need alone, Liverpool found itself becoming a pioneer of social reform, helped by a series of special Acts of Parliament and bye-laws. Having stated his case so forcibly the good Dr Duncan was made Liverpool's, and Britain's, first Medical Officer of Health in 1847. One of his first acts was to mount a campaign against unfit housing. No less than 5,000 of the town's 14,085 inhabited cellars were condemned out of hand and cleared of their residents.

The link between dirt and disease had already been established by Dr Duncan and others. Liverpool at that time was the archetypal 'dirty old town' whose residents must have been rather smelly. To eliminate dirt, a plentiful supply of water was needed, something which

Liverpool simply did not have. Water was piped from two local wells by rival companies but in totally inadequate quantities. It was often turned on for only 15 or 30 minutes on alternate days and frequently at inconvenient times such as late at night or very early in the morning. In the poorer parts of town whole courts would have to share one standpipe. Inevitably the same water was used time and time again. Personal hygiene and cleanliness were nigh impossible. Conditions were ideal for the spread of disease.

Liverpool had to wait until 1857 before it had the 'luxury' of a continuous and plentiful supply of pure water. In the meantime, an Act of 1846 compelled the Council to provide adequate sewerage facilities for all streets in the town. This led to the appointment in 1847 of James Newlands as Liverpool's, and Britain's, first Borough Engineer to deal with the town's sewerage and water problems.

Pioneered by Kitty Wilkinson who, in 1833, threw open her kitchen as a place where cholera sufferers could wash their clothes, the first public washhouse in the country was opened in 1842. Subsequently, these were set up in working class areas throughout the town; the last one was closed down fairly recently, a victim of the electric washing machine now to be found in nearly every home.

This was 'the other Liverpool' of 1846, the year that the Prince Consort opened the ultimate expression of the port's maritime greatness...Albert Dock.

The rise and rise of the Port of Liverpool

The Cunard-White Star Line's RMS 'Mauretania' II, 1,000-plus luxury passenger liner, built across the River Mersey from Liverpool at Cammell Laird, Birkenhead, for the transatlantic service. The biggest ship ever built in England up to that time, she was launched in 1938 and her maiden voyage the following year took her from Liverpool to New York. With the outbreak of the Second World War, Mauretania was requisitioned as a troopship, sailing over 500,000 miles and carrying over 350,000 troops. In 1946 she returned to Liverpool to be re-fitted once again by Cammell Laird for the transatlantic service. This did not last long and she spent her remaining years cruising in the Mediterranean and the tropics before finally being sold for scrap in 1965.

In the beginning...

As every local schoolchild knows, the 'town' or, to be more precise, 'borough', of Liverpool was founded by King John in 1207. The King had spotted its potential as a port of embarkation to wage war on the Irish and was keen to encourage the growth of his new town. Up until that time Liverpool had been a tiny fishing village with an agricultural hinterland, so small that it didn't even rate a mention in the Doomsday Survey of 1086. The 'pool' of Liverpool was little more than a marshy inlet which meandered where Paradise Street and Whitechapel are today, finishing up where the entrance to the Mersey Tunnel to Birkenhead is situated.

The town grew steadily but unremarkably over the next three centuries. During the 17th century the pace noticeably quickened. Trade with Ireland increased. Liverpool had shaken off its previous status as a 'creek', overtaken its old rival Chester due to the silting up of the River Dee, and been made a port in its own right.

However, by the 1650s trade was virtually non-existent due to the troubles in Ireland again. The whole of that country was in ruin. Over 600,000 people had been killed, as had most of its horses and cattle, and that was on top of plague, famine and emigration. Liverpool had to look elsewhere for her livelihood. That 'elsewhere' was across the Atlantic Ocean.

"Westward look the land is bright."

By 1666, Liverpool had entered the oceanic trade and her ships began sailing to the West Indies, and soon the American colonies, returning with sugar, tobacco and timber. From then on Liverpool never looked back. By the turn of the century trade with the colonies was well-established with over 25 ships sailing for, or returning from, America, in a year, although a serious 'blip' was caused by the American War of Independence (1775-1783) and the loss of the American colonies.

Liverpool 1797.

At that time Liverpool, a town of 24 principal streets, could boast over 100 ships and 1100 seamen. Those ships had to sail into the tidal basin of The Pool to unload their cargoes onto the quaysides; very inconvenient and inefficient. And what to do with them in the winter? Traditionally, ships had been hauled up onto the beach above the high water mark. But now there was a shortage of land with all available ground taken up with another local industry - shipbuilding.

Ship-building on the banks of the Mersey.

Shipbuilding was an important part of the Liverpool economy, seriously diminished when Jesse Hartley served notice to quit on the last major yard in 1841 so that construction of Albert Dock could begin. The King's and Queen's Docks had already pushed shipbuilding further south until, by the end of the 19th century, it was completely driven over the other side of the Mersey to Birkenhead where it remains to this day, a victim of the success of Liverpool as a port that demanded more and more docks and quaysides.

Liverpool builds its first dock.

If the port was to grow, something had to be done, and fast. The answer was Liverpool's first dock. In 1709 an Act of Parliament was obtained to build a four-acre dock open for three hours each tide and with the capacity to berth 100 ships at any one time. The cost would be £10,000. A dock was built but it was not that one. Thomas Steers was brought from London and produced a plan for a completely different dock. Known as the 'Old Dock', it would be built virtually into the River Mersey and it would cost half as much again as the original plan.

Opened in 1715, but not completed until 1720, the Old Dock, the first commercial wet dock in the world, was a runaway success. Daniel Defoe, author of Robinson Crusoe, described Liverpool as "...one of the wonders of Britain..." and was especially taken with "...the great wet dock..." Such was the growth in Liverpool's trade that, within 20 years, the Old Dock was too small.

Ships of shame

And the 18th century had ushered in a trade of a different kind for Liverpool - 'black gold', the 'Africa Trade', the 'Triangular Trade' or, to give it its proper description, the slave trade. It was this grisly trade which was to engage Liverpool for more than a century and in which, for a time, she came to hold world domination. It has been suggested that Liverpool ships carried half the world trade in slaves from Africa to America and the West Indies. In one year alone, 1792, Liverpool

Liverpool slaveship c1780

ships transported an estimated 40,000 slaves; five years later, Bristol was to send out 5 slaveships, London 17 and Liverpool, 134. On top of this Liverpool had long been immersed in privateering, which was little more than licensed piracy, albeit directed at the enemies of the Crown.

By the time the 18th century had drawn to a close, Liverpool's population had soared to 80,000, up from a start-of-the-century tally of a mere 5,000. The number of new docks had increased to keep pace with the boom in trade. Thomas Steers had added a Custom House and a dry dock and pier to his Old Dock and began constructing Salthouse Dock in 1736. George's Dock came along in 1771 followed by King's Dock in 1788 and Queen's Dock in 1796; as part of the celebrations for the opening of Queen's Dock, bull-baiting was organised in the dock basin, prior to it being flooded with water. Liverpool was well on the way to having a proper system of docks. In the process she had become the most important port and largest town in the country, London apart. Surely things couldn't get any better, could they? Well, yes they could, and on a scale beyond anybody's wildest imaginings.

Liverpool always had the knack of exploiting a new market when an old one had come to an end. When the *Kitty's Amelia* sailed up the Mersey in 1807 with Liverpool Captain Hugh 'mind your eye' Crow at the helm, it marked the final, legal, slaving voyage. One can picture the merchants pacing the quaysides and wringing their hands in despair when Parliament that year put an end to this evil, but profitable, trade. The holds of their ships had carried 50,000 of these poor souls the previous year alone. What were they to do now?

Custom House.

Statue of a young emigrant family on Riverside Walkway.

Give me your poor...

They needn't have worried for soon their ships would be carrying human cargo of a different kind - emigrants. The greatest mass migration in history was underway, fuelled by America's inexhaustible demand for labour and wages that were about five times higher than in Europe. In the epic days of emigration 200,000 emigrants set sail from Liverpool to American each year. A luxury trans-atlantic cruise it was not. Indeed, one emigrant manual of 1851 warned its readers that they would be "...as captive in their vessel as an African in a slaveship." However, it did not warn them that conditions could be worse for them than for slaves: the captain of a slaveship had a money incentive for keeping his 'cargo' alive and in good condition.

It was a trade dominated by Liverpool and it has been estimated that, between 1830 and 1930, nine million emigrants from Britain, Ireland and Europe had set sail from Liverpool to begin a new life in America.

The Port of Liverpool was also given a massive boost by the removal of trade restrictions such as the abolition in 1833 of the East India Company's trading monopoly with the Far East and, coinciding with the formal opening of Albert Dock, the repeal of the Corn Laws in 1846. During Queen Victoria's reign, Liverpool ships were free to trade virtually wherever in the world they wished. As a Liverpool guidebook of 1852 remarked – "...the ships and products of Liverpool are to be found in every port of the world accessible to merchantmen."

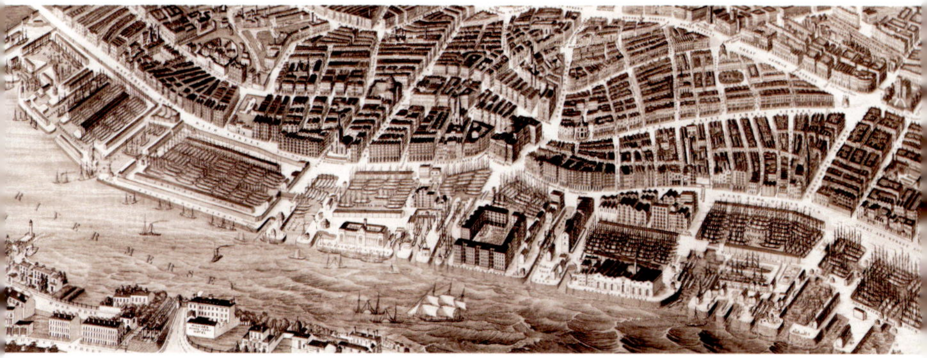

River Mersey and Liverpool docks, early 1850's.

On the home front, Britain's 'industrial revolution' was in full swing. A network of canals and railways linked the industrial heartlands of Lancashire, Yorkshire and the Midlands to Liverpool. The port was sitting pretty for an export trade that was soon to nearly double that of its nearest rival, London.

The gargantuan dock wall now stretched for miles along the eastern bank of the River Mersey, protecting the ever-expanding docks and quaysides. Herman Melville, the great American author of *Moby Dick*, was mightily impressed. He likened it to the Great Wall of China and the pyramids of the Egyptian pharoahs; in his eyes it was no less than one of the great wonders of the world.

The picture was one of endless opportunity for Liverpool and its merchants and ship-owners. Befitting a town very much on the up, it began to erect buildings that reflected its soaring wealth and status as, arguably, the second city in the British Empire. The noblest of these was St George's Hall, under construction at the same time as Albert Dock, and dubbed, with typical Liverpudlian modesty, 'the greatest neo-classical building in the world'. There were many others - whole streets of them. In a swathe stretching from Albert Dock and the Pier Head, through Castle Street, Dale Street and Victoria Street to William Brown Street, you will see fine buildings galore, survivors of the great Victorian construction boom. There can be little doubt that for much of the 19th century Liverpool must have resembled a giant building site.

St George's Hall, Lime Street c.1890s.

By the time of Jesse Hartley's death in 1860, with the exception of the private railway port of Garston, the entire dock system on both sides of the river, including Birkenhead docks which had been established to challenge Liverpool's monopoly, had come under the control of the Mersey Docks & Harbour Board, set up in 1858. In his 36 years as Dock Engineer, Hartley had spent over £5m providing more than half of Liverpool's 140 acres of docks and ten miles of quaysides.

The Cunard liner 'Scythia' anchored off Albert Dock during the last quarter of the 19th century.

Whilst the oceanic cargo trade at that time was still largely being carried in sailing ships, growing numbers of steamships were involved in the coastal and cross-channel trade. By value, nearly half the country's export trade, and about one-third of the import trade, was passing through Liverpool.

King Cotton

In terms of value – but not volume, for grain was the chief commodity – one trade dominated the port during the second half of the 19th century: cotton. The port had been importing cotton for most of the 18th century but during the 19th century Liverpool achieved world domination and reigned supreme as 'King Cotton'. In 1820, some 111,000 tons came into the port. By 1850 this had grown to 360,000 tons and, by the 1890s, 660,000 tons were being shipped in each year. For many years, up to 90% of the country's total cotton imports came to Liverpool. These reached their peak in the 1911-1912 season, when 5,230,000 bales were imported, mostly to Liverpool. At that time, Liverpool was the largest cotton importing market in the world.

Bales of cotton arrived in Liverpool from the Americas, India, Egypt and Brazil and were stored in dockland warehouses, including Albert Dock, before being transported to other manufacturing centres. Yarn, textiles and finished cotton goods were then sent back to the port for worldwide export in Liverpool ships. And, to complete the circle, Liverpool merchants, first in the open air on Exchange Flags behind the Town Hall and then from the floor of the Cotton Exchange, regulated prices and ensured future supplies.

Cotton is no longer imported into the United Kingdom but Liverpool still remains a force to be reckoned with - over 60% of the world's cotton trade is said to be purchased and sold under Liverpool Cotton Association (International Cotton Association since 2004) Bylaws.

There was no stopping Liverpool. Between 1860 and 1890, the net registered tonnage of shipping doubled from 4.7m to 9.6m and doubled again to reach 19m by 1914. And, to keep pace with this expansion of trade, new docks were continuously being commissioned – more than 145 acres on the Liverpool side of the river alone between 1862 and 1927, an acreage equivalent to nearly nineteen Albert Docks.

Locally manufactured steam locos being loaded for export at Birkenhead docks.

The lean years - the decline of a great port

But nothing lasts forever and, with the outbreak of the First World War, the storm clouds were beginning to gather over the Port of Liverpool. The war caused considerable disruption and loss of trade and profits for the port. Dock workers had enlisted in droves in the armed forces. This, coupled with the slowdown in modernising the docks (there was a chronic shortage of cranes and virtually no electricity throughout the entire dock estate), the slide in the fortunes of many Merseyside shipping companies as a direct result of the war, and increased competition from overseas ports, meant that Liverpool had a lot of catching up to do after the war ended in 1918. The one bright spot was the grain trade which was doing so well that new mills and silos were springing up in Birkenhead.

Cunard's 'Aquitania' berthed alongside Riverside Railway Station. Liverpool's domination of the transatlantic liner trade had been on the slide since the White Star Line decided to move its express liners to Southampton in 1907. The last White Star liners eventually left Liverpool in 1936. The final Cunarder left in 1966 and the following year saw the departure of Canadian Pacific, marking the end of 127 continuous years of the port's involvement in the transatlantic liner trade.

The first steps in the long road to recovery were made when the Dock Board in that year began the electrification of the dock estate. The Liverpool shipping companies, who had lost over 1.5m tons of shipping, which would cost some £280 million to replace, tried hard to re-establish their markets. Their efforts were thwarted with the onset of a world depression in 1929. This lasted until 1933 and hit Merseyside hard. The previous twenty years had been difficult ones for Liverpool and to add to her woes another war in Europe was looming.

With the outbreak of World War Two in 1939, Liverpool quickly became the most important port in the nation's war effort and thus was an inevitable target for the bombers of Hitler's Luftwaffe. The first bombs fell on the Mersey's docklands in July 1940 and reached their peak with the May blitz of 1941 at the end of which one-third of the 144 berths had been put out of action; after that the city was mostly spared from further air raids.

HMS Whimbrel from a painting by Edward D Walker. Royal Navy corvettes such as this were moored in Albert Dock throughout World War II and played a crucial role in Britain winning the Battle of the Atlantic, the war's longest continuous campaign.

The aerial bombardments had a crippling effect on the port, closing it completely for the equivalent of 54 days. Among key port buildings to take direct hits were the Dock Board's domed headquarters, the beautiful Georgian Custom House and Albert Dock; Jesse Hartley's monumental dock walls had largely withstood the onslaught. And, of course, much warehousing, berthing space, and shipping at those berths, had been destroyed.

Liverpool had also played the key role in the long-running Battle of the Atlantic. A basement room in an office building close to the Pier Head, known as The Fortress, housed the Combined Headquarters of the Western Approaches where the planning of the Battle of the Atlantic took place. No fewer than 1,285 convoys, the largest of which comprised 60 ships, arrived in the port from North America and Canada carrying troops and supplies vital for the war effort.

For a variety of reasons, reconstruction of the battered port was a painfully slow process which did not get underway until the 1950's. The flexibility demanded by the changing patterns of world trade was a lesson Liverpool had learned the hard way during the inter-war years and it was to stand her in good stead in the post-war recovery period.

The fortunes of the port started to fall after 1966, compounded by a number of factors. A series of strikes by seamen, dockers and car workers had left Merseyside with the worst labour relations image in the country. Liverpool was losing trade to other, more cost-efficient, British and European ports and foreign shipping lines. And the changing patterns of trade, and the way in which that trade was carried, meant that Liverpool was on the 'wrong' side of the country for the containerised traffic now coming from continental Europe.

Royal Seaforth Dock. Liverpool remains Britain's premier port for the North American container trade and serves over 100 other non-EU destinations.

'Containerise or die' was the message of the 60s. It was a message Liverpool heard, loud and clear. A container berth was operational at Gladstone Dock from 1967 and in 1971 the £50 million Royal Seaforth Dock offering container, grain and timber terminals, opened.

Another, less positive, scenario was taking place at around the same time. The late 60s and early 70s were years when the port was in financial crisis and staring closure in the face. The Board was unable to meet its debts and Parliament passed a special Act which replaced the old Harbour Board with a new Mersey Docks & Harbour Company in 1971. The following year the new company shut down all the docks south of the Pier Head, including Albert Dock.

The downward spiral nevertheless continued through to the early 1980s despite a number of positive developments such as a new Freightliner rail terminal at Seaforth, now developed into a Euro-Rail terminal for Channel Tunnel trains and domestic rail traffic. Cargo through the port had plummeted to 9.3 million tonnes by 1982.

A great port re-born

A major rationalisation plan which involved the wholesale shedding of excess manpower, changes to the dockers' notorious working practices and a ground-breaking two-year pay deal, coupled with an entrepreneurial business development philosophy, seemed to do the trick. By 1984 Mersey Docks had made a modest profit of £800,000 on a turnover of about £50 million. The tide had turned.

Liverpool Freeport, the largest and foremost U.K. freeport, was also launched in 1984. The second half of the 1980s and the 1990s saw much diversification. For example, the Kent ports of Sheerness and Chatham were acquired, as was the major container shipping line on the Irish Sea. Mersey Docks also operates port terminals in Dublin, Belfast and Cardiff and its port management consultancy arm is the largest in the U.K. and operates throughout the world.

In 1997, handling a record volume of nearly 31 million tonnes of cargo, Mersey Docks turned in profits of £48 million on a £168 million turnover and even managed to invest over £50 million in expanding the Port and Freeport.

Mersey Docks entered the new millennium in much better health. In 2003, a record year with nearly 32 million tonnes being handled, it notched up profits of £53.7 million on a turnover of £297 million. In the previous year the Lancashire port of Heysham was acquired and the £25 million Twelve Quays Ferry Terminal opened, ushering in new passenger and freight services to Dublin and Belfast.

In 2005 the Mersey Docks & Harbour Company was acquired by Peel Holdings Ltd., whose vast portfolio includes Liverpool John Lennon Airport and the Manchester Ship Canal. Peel has many ambitious plans for the Port including a £350m deep water container terminal and the multi-£billion Liverpool Waters and Wirral Waters schemes.

The first decade of the 21st century has certainly demonstrated that the Port of Liverpool is able to hold her own and indeed prosper in the face of fierce competition and difficult world markets.

The 3,000-passenger "Crown Princess" berthed at the Cruise Liner Terminal which opened at the Pier Head in 2007.

WELCOME TO
ALBERT DOCK
Welcome
COSTA

Visitor Guide to Albert Dock

Every effort has been made to ensure that the information in this guide was correct at the time of going to print (May 2013). However, before setting off for Albert Dock, you are advised to visit the Dock's website – ***www.albertdock.com*** *– for any information updates, especially so far as events are concerned.*

General

Albert Dock is open to visitors from 10.00 am daily. However, the opening times of individual attractions and businesses can vary. General admission is free although certain attractions charge an admission fee, as do some special exhibitions. For up-to-the-minute information about the Dock's attractions, special events, opening hours etc., visit their websites – addresses are given in the 'Useful Websites' section on page 89.

The best place to start planning your visit is the Albert Dock website – ***www.albertdock.com*** This includes detailed information about restaurants, cafés and coffee shops where you can eat and drink at Albert Dock as well as all the places to visit and things to see and do at the Dock. You will also find money-off vouchers which you can download. Detailed 'How to find us' travel directions are there too.

Liverpool's main Tourist Information Centre can be found at Albert Dock, in Anchor Courtyard. Here you will be able to pick up a map, find out what's on at the Dock that day and buy a guidebook or memento of your visit. There is also a Tourist Information Centre at Liverpool John Lennon Airport. For general visitor information about Liverpool, go to: ***www.visitliverpool.com***

Parking

Car parking immediately adjacent to Albert Dock is sparse and limited to 'pay and display' parking on the left as you enter the main entrance and in bays opposite Britannia Pavilion. But be warned! Infringing the Dock's parking provisions can result in heavy penalties. A large multi-storey car park next door to the Liverpool Arena and Convention Centre also caters for visitors to the nearby Albert Dock. Other multi-storey car parks can be found just a short walk across the dock road in the Liverpool One Shopping Centre and at John Lewis.

A number of parking bays have been set aside in the Dock's 'pay and display' areas for disabled visitors.

Coach parking is available at King's Dock, adjacent to Albert Dock. Coaches can also drop off passengers at Albert Dock Gate and Gower Street bus stop. For information about group visits go to the Albert Dock website – www.albertdock.com

The Dock's main visitor attractions

From culture both high and low, you'll find it all at the Dock. It's possible to spend a whole day and more exploring Tate Liverpool, the Merseyside Maritime Museum, the International Slavery Museum and The Beatles Story Exhibition and still run out of time. And, if you take in Albert Dock's next door neighbour, the not-to-be-missed Museum of Liverpool, which opened in 2011, you'll need two days to cram in everything. See also pages 90-95.

Shop at the Dock

Shopping at Albert Dock is quite different from anywhere else in Liverpool. For a start you won't find any of the usual stores that makes our high streets so predictable. Instead, there is a small selection of interesting speciality shops, a number of which cater specifically for visitors to Liverpool in general and Albert Dock in particular. For Liverpool, Beatles, football or maritime mementos, or gifts that are a little bit out of the ordinary, Albert Dock is the place to find them. Here's a brief guide:

Britannia Pavilion/Anchor Courtyard:

Visitor Information Centre (Liverpool-related books and souvenirs)
Impressions of Liverpool (Albert Dock, Liverpool & football souvenirs)
Nauticalia (wide range of nautical gifts and instruments, clothing etc)
Fab Four Store (Beatles Story giftshop-Beatles memorabilia, books etc)

Colonnades

Beeartistic (Modern and classical oil paintings and educational toys)
Annabel's Accessories (Ladies' fashion accessories)
Quay Confectionery (Sweets and confectionery)
Liverpool Pictures (Modern and historic local pictures, postcards etc)
Nature's Treasure (Gifts, ornaments, semi-precious stones, jewellery)
With Love From Liverpool (Novelties, pictures, cards and souvenirs)
The Gift Company (Gifts, ornaments and small items of furniture)
Treatment Express (Range of beauty treatments, face painting and gifts)
Tate Liverpool Shop (Books, cards, art-related and Liverpool gifts)

Maritime Museum (Ground floor)

Wide range of souvenirs, books, postcards and fair trade gifts.

Places to eat & drink

Albert Dock offers a wide range of restaurants, cafés, coffee shops and bars, most with splendid quayside views. Remember too that many of them stay open into the evening, and some into the early hours. Albert Dock, which can perhaps boast the city's highest celebrity count, is a great place to go for a good night out.

Edward Pavilion:

Gusto (Italian / Mediterranean cuisine - pizza, pasta, seafood, grills)
Blue Bar & Grill (Grill restaurant)

Atlantic Pavilion:

Revolution Bar & Restaurant (Burgers, pizza, wraps, salads, steaks etc)
Miller & Carter Steakhouse (Steaks, chicken, pasta, fish, burgers etc))
Spice Lounge (Contemporary Indian cuisine, Tandoori oven)

Britannia Pavilion:

Circo (Classic, salads, pasta, pizza, sandwiches)
Costa Coffee (Coffee shop with outdoor terrace)
Vinea (Wine bar, coffee shop and delicatessen)
Pan Am Bar & Restaurant (Steaks, fish & chips, chicken, duck, seafood, pasta)
What's Cooking (American diner-style, burgers, ribs, fishcakes, chicken, steaks, nachos etc)
Starbucks coffee shop (entrance in Anchor Courtyard or from within The Beatles Story's Fab4Store)

The Colonnades

Funky Shake Bar (milk shakes, smoothies and other refreshments)
Gallery Café serving breakfasts and light lunches. Quayside seating.
La Crepe Rit (French-style café: croissants, savoury gallettes, steaks etc)
Tate Café (Breakfasts, soup, sandwiches, pastries, hot meals and more)

Elsewhere at Albert Dock

Maritime Museum: Maritime Dining Rooms – Regional, modern and affordable food. Also Quayside Café – coffee shop with free wi-fi.
The Pumphouse (Pub with classic British food)

Hotels at Albert Dock, or a few minutes' walk away

Holiday Inn Express, Britannia Pavilion, Albert Dock: 135 en-suite bedrooms. Complimentary buffet breakfast. Restaurant, lounge and bar area overlooking the Dock. www.holidayinnexpressliverpool.com
Premier Inn Hotel, Britannia Pavilion, Albert Dock: 186 en-suite bedrooms. Lounge and breakfast area overlooking the Dock.
www.premierinn.com/en/hotel/LIVPLI/liverpool-albert-dock
Jury's Inn, Keel Wharf: 310 rooms. http://liverpoolhotels.jurysinns.com/
Staybridge Suites Keel Wharf: 130 rooms. www.staybridge.com
Hilton Liverpool Liverpool One. 215 rooms. www.hilton.co.uk/liverpool
Ibis Hotel Liverpool: Wapping. 127 rooms. www.ibishotel.com

Disabled visitors

Disabled visitors are well-catered for at Albert Dock and its various attractions. Despite being a docklands heritage location abounding with York flagstones and cobblestones, wheelchair users can still get around conveniently. The individual major attractions at the Dock are all well geared to welcoming disabled visitors. Detailed information can be found on the Albert Dock website: www.albertdock.com

Dogs / Cycles

Apart from assistance dogs, dogs are not allowed on the dock estate. Whilst Albert Dock welcomes visiting cyclists, riding a cycle around the quaysides is prohibited on safety grounds. The same rule applies to skates, skateboards etc.

Tours

The Yellow Duckmarine: Frequent departures in World War Two landing craft from Gower Street bus stop. Approximately one hour tour takes in popular city centre sights and historic waterfront
Booking office – Anchor Courtyard.
www.theyellowduckmarine.co.uk T: 0151 708 7799

The Yellow Boat Cruise: A 40-minute pleasure cruise of Albert, Salthouse and other historic south docks, with live commentary. Booking details as above.

Magical Mystery Tour: 1hr 45mins tour of Penny Lane, Strawberry Field and other places associated with The Beatles and people who were close to them. Departs at 11.30am and 2pm daily. Additional tours also take place at peak times. Bookings can be made at the Albert Dock Visitor Information Centre, Anchor Courtyard.
www.cavernclub.org T: 0151 151 233 2459

Useful websites

Albert Dock – www.albertdock.com
The Beatles Story – www.beatlesstory.com
Maritime Museum – www.liverpoolmuseums.org.uk/maritime
International Slavery Museum – www.liverpoolmuseums.org.uk/ism
Tate Liverpool – www.tate.org.uk/liverpool
Museum of Liverpool – www.liverpoolmuseums.org.uk/mol
Yellow Duckmarine – www.theyellowduckmarine.co.uk
Yellow Boat Cruise – as above
Magical Mystery Tour – www.cavernclub.org/the-magical-mystery-tour
Open Top Bus Tours – www.city-sightseeing.com
Open Eye Photography Gallery – www.openeye.org.uk
Blue Badge Guided Tours of Liverpool, – www.showmeliverpool.com
Echo Arena Liverpool events – www.echoarena.com/index.asp
BT Convention Centre – www.accliverpool.com
Liverpool One – www.liverpool-one.com
Liverpool Visitor Information website – www.visitliverpool.com

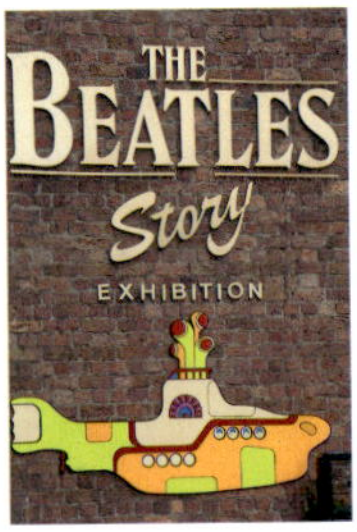

The Beatles Story. Arguably the greatest pop phenomenon of the 20th century, the Beatles are synonymous with Liverpool, the city of their birth. In the arched basement of Britannia Pavilion, reminiscent of the legendary Cavern Club where the Beatles honed their skills in 274 performances, is The Beatles Story which opened in 1990. The Beatles Story is literally that...the amazing 'rags to riches' story of The Beatles from their childhood days through to their break-up and the pursuit of individual careers. This is done by way of a series of rooms including the office of the *Mersey Beat* newspaper, Hamburg's Reeperbahn, the Cavern club, Sgt Pepper/Yellow Submarine, a Lennon 'White Room' etc. Some of the key features of the Casbah Coffee Club, one of the Beatles' very early haunts, were added in 1999.

An extension, opened in 2008, effectively doubled the size of The Beatles Story. A gallery, *Going Solo,* focuses on the individual Beatles' solo careers. A hands-on, inter-active Discovery Zone will be of special interest to families and school groups. Creature comforts are catered for in the Starbucks café and chill-out area whilst a well-stocked Fab4Store completes the visitor experience.

To get the most out of your visit, opt for the 'Living History' tour, narrated by John Lennon's half-sister Julia. You'll also hear the voices of Brian Epstein, Paul McCartney, Allan Williams, Cynthia Lennon and George Martin as they tell you about the group's rise to fame. The tour is available in eight languages. For the latest information, booking tickets on-line, browsing the on-line shop etc., check out - *www.beatlesstory.com*

For fans of the Fab Four, a visit to The Beatles Story is essential. Even general visitors to Liverpool and the Dock will find it very entertaining and a visit is highly recommended.

): Left – A flavour of Hamburg's Reeperbahn and the Star Club. Right – Your admission ticket for The Beatles ·ry gets you into its Beatles Story Pier Head attraction at the Mersey Ferries Terminal, 10 minutes' walk away. ntre: Embryo Beatles, The Quarrymen and their guitars/The Beatles in the recording studio/Hessy's Music Store, erpool, where the Beatles bought their instruments. Bottom: Opposite page: Psychedelia, the Sgt Pepper and low Submarine days. Left – The atmospheric Lennon White Room. Right – Recreation of the Cavern club's stage.

Merseyside Maritime Museum featuring Seized! and The International Slavery Museum (in the same building)

Both museums are part of National Museums Liverpool and have international standing. The Merseyside Maritime Museum tells the story of one of the world's greatest ports and the people who used it. There are two museums in one building – in addition to the Maritime Museum, the former warehouse is also the home of the International Slavery Museum, opened in 2007. And best of all, admission to both museums is free! They occupy an entire block of Albert Dock as well as extensive quaysides, graving docks and other buildings, so allow plenty of time to get the most out of your visit.

Ground Floor: Information desk; gift shop; toilets and lockers; café with free wi-fi access; 'Liverpool: World Gateway', a display of ship models and shipping companies.

Basement: When Britain's slave trade ended in 1807, Liverpool entered, and soon dominated, the trade in transporting emigrants to the New World. That story is told in the Emigration Gallery. Seized!, a permanent gallery, features the work of HM Revenue and Customs.

First Floor: 'Titanic, Lusitania and the Forgotten Empress'. The stories of three of the biggest tragedies in maritime history. 'The Forgotten Empress'? She was Canadian Pacific's Liverpool-Quebec liner *Empress of Ireland* which sank in the St Lawrence river in 1914 with the loss of 840 passengers, even more than the *Titanic*. There is an enormous and very beautiful model of *Titanic* on display in this gallery. During World War II the Battle of the Atlantic was master-minded from Liverpool and a special gallery tells that epic story. Another section portrays what 'Life at Sea' was all about.

Second Floor: 'Art and the Sea' displays fine examples of maritime art, ships' figureheads and some of the museum's vast collection of ship models. There's also a gallery displaying a changing programme of exhibitions. The Maritime Archives and Library can also be found here.

Third Floor (and former Dock Traffic Office): International Slavery Museum. During the 18th century Liverpool rose to become Europe's premier slave-trading port – its ships carried an estimated 1.5 million African slaves so it is fitting that this museum should be located here, just a stone's throw from the historic graving docks where slaveships were once repaired and fitted out. The adjoining former Dock Traffic Office is being developed as a slavery resource centre.

Fourth Floor: Maritime Dining Rooms – one of only ten restaurants listed in the *Michelin Guide Great Britain & Ireland*. As a bonus there are superb views of the Pier Head and Albert Dock from this floor and it is one of the few places where you can see the Dock's original cast iron roof structure. Also on this floor is a theatre for presentations and conferences – the museum is a popular, out-of-the-ordinary conference and meeting venue.

Elsewhere: Don't miss the Piermaster's House, offices and cooperage, historic ships, 18th century graving docks and quaysides.

Opening times: Open daily 10am-5pm (Piermaster's house closes at 4.30pm). Maritime Archives and Library: Open Tuesday-Thursday 10.30am-4.30pm. Museum is closed from 2pm on 24th December and all day on 25th/26th December and 1st January.

Enquiries: T: 0151 478 4499
www.liverpoolmuseums.org.uk/maritime/visitor

Opposite page (clockwise): Builder's model of the 'unsinkable' Liverpool-registered White Star liner 'Titanic'; ship's figurehead; endangered species featured in Seized!; display in emigration gallery; Nazi war objects in Battle of the Atlantic Gallery.
This page (clockwise): Emblem of the Cunard Steamship Company; Liverpool slaveship; reconstruction of slave plantation; manacles and other gruesome 'hardware' displayed in the International Slavery Museum. Some of the models of ships built by Isambard Kingdom Brunel in the 'Art and the Sea' gallery.

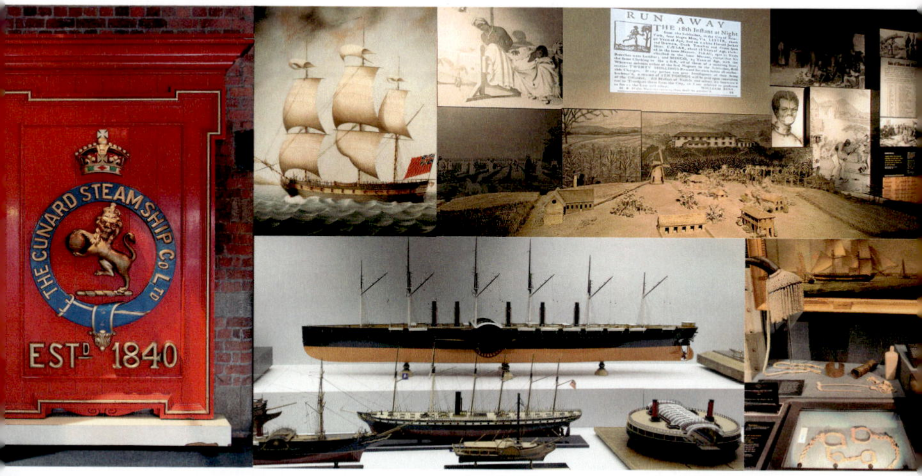

Tate Liverpool

The opening of Tate Liverpool in 1988 as the home of the 'National Collection of Modern Art in the North of England' was a landmark event for the city and put Liverpool on the international cultural map.

The Gallery showcases two main types of exhibits: art selected from the national Tate Collection, and special exhibitions of contemporary art which bring together works loaned from other collections both public and private and both national and international. Over 150 different exhibitions and displays by hundreds of different artists have been shown since the Gallery opened.

The original conversion from a derelict mid-19th century dockland warehouse into a modern art gallery was undertaken by the world-renowned architect Sir James Sterling (1926-1992) who, co-incidentally, studied architecture at Liverpool University.

Encouraged by the number of visitors who flocked to the Gallery during its first decade, major additional gallery space was added in 1998. The foyer area was remodelled in 2007 in preparation for Tate Liverpool to play a major role in the city's year as European Capital of Culture in 2008.

The Gallery shows the challenging variety of objects that are included in the field of modern and contemporary art: photography, printmaking, video, performance and installation as well as painting and sculpture.

Sir Jacob Epstein's monumental alabaster statue 'Jacob and the Angel' dominates the foyer. Dating from 1940-1, the sculpture was once considered highly risque but today shocks no one.

Displays are housed on four floors of the building. On the ground floor (pictured right) which is mainly given over to an entrance foyer and visitor services, there is an excellent book and giftshop and the Tate Liverpool Café. This is open during gallery hours for breakfast, lunch, afternoon tea or simply for a coffee break at any time.

Admission to Tate Liverpool is free although admission charges usually apply to special exhibitions.

Gallery, Café & Shop Hours: Daily 10.00 am – 17.50 pm from (approx) Easter until 6 October and 10.00 am – 17.00 pm 7 October until (approx) Easter. Closed on Good Friday and 24/26 December. For precise information, 'phone or check details on-line:

Enquiries: T: 0151 702 7400 / www.tate.org.uk/liverpool

Top three rows: Installation images of DLA Piper Series: This is Sculpture (2009-2013) – the third row shows the gallery designed by fashion designer Wayne Hemingway and his son Jack.
Bottom row: Special exhibition – 'Afro Modern: Journeys through the Black Atlantic'. The 4th floor galleries give visitors the chance to see the original cast iron roof construction...as well as World War II shrapnel damage.

Albert Dock at-a-glance

1837	Jesse Hartley submits his plans for Albert Dock.
1841	Construction begins.
1846	Prince Albert officially opens Albert Dock.
1920	From now on, virtually no commercial shipping activity.
1952	Albert Dock given Grade 1 Listed Building status.
1972	Albert Dock, and entire redundant South Docks closed, the whole dock system becomes tidal and soon silts up.
1976	Albert given Conservation Area status.
1983	Work begins by Arrowcroft/Merseyside Development Corporation to regenerate Albert.
1984	First phase of redeveloped dock opens.
2002	Final phase of undeveloped space completed by Arrowcroft.

- Original cost: £514,475 8s 1d – the warehouses alone cost some £358,000. Total cost, including land acquisition – £782,265.
- Refurbishment between 1983 and 2003 cost in excess of £100 million.

Materials used included:

- 23.5 million bricks
- 47,000 tons of mortar
- 13,729 piles of timber – equivalent to 48 miles

- Warehousing – 1.29 million square feet.
- Enclosed water area – 7.75 acres.
- First dock warehousing designed to be fireproof.
- First structure in Great Britain to be constructed principally of cast iron, wrought iron, stone and brick. Roof was possibly first stressed-skin structure of any kind, discounting the violin!
- West and North of Albert built on quicksand. Dock rises and falls with each tide.
- Cast iron columns are 15 feet high by 12.5 feet in circumference.
- Estimated number of visitors each year – in excess of four million.
- Albert Dock is the UK's largest group of Grade 1 Listed buildings.

The award-winning Albert Dock

1986 European Gold Medal for the Preservation of Historic Monuments awarded by the FVS Foundation, Hamburg.

1987 Civic Trust Award – Merseyside Maritime Museum.

1988 MANWEB 'Medallion Award'. Premier award for homes achieving the highest all-electric standards.
BETA award won by 'The Wharf' restaurant for the efficient use of energy in commercial buildings
Royal Institute of Chartered Surveyors – 'Highly Commended' in their 'Inner City Awards'.
Royal Institute of British Architects – 'Regional Award' in recognition of the outstanding achievement for the conservation of the Merseyside Maritime Museum's building.
Lighting Industry Federation – The Tate Gallery was 'Highly Commended' in the 'National Lighting Awards'.
British Tourist Authority – overall winner of the 'Come To Britain' trophy.
North West Tourist Board – winner of 'Large Tourist Attraction' category in 'Best of the North West' awards.

1989 Royal Institute of British Architects – The Tate Gallery won a 'National Architecture' award (one of 16 in the UK).
Crown Berger – Tate Gallery won Colouring our Lives" award.
'National Heritage Museum of the Year' award – won by The Tate Gallery as 'The Best Museum of Fine Art'.
Association for Business Sponsorship of the Arts – award to the Tate Gallery. The Tate also won a number of awards for its opening television advertising campaign.
Institute of Structural Engineers – Albert Dock was first-time winner of their 'Structural Heritage' award.

1990 North West Tourist Board – 'New Year's Honours for Tourism' (Large Attraction category).

1991 Royal Institution of Chartered Surveyors – 'Urban Renewal' award.
North West Tourist Board – Tourist Attraction of the Year (Best Large Attraction).
North West Tourist Board – 'Come To Britain' award for The Beatles Story's contribution to the tourist industry,

1992 North West Tourist Board Tourist Attraction of the Year (Best Large Attraction)

1993 British Urban Regeneration Association (BURA) Best Practice Award.
North West Tourist Board – Tourist Attraction of the Year 3rd place (Best Large Attraction)

2000 Awarded the 'Millennium Marque' to commemorate environmental excellence. Albert Dock was the only project in Merseyside to receive this award.

Above: Bird's eye view of Albert Dock in the 1880s. On its left is Canning Dock and, to its right, is Duke's Dock (see also below right) and King's Dock with the warehouses of Wapping Dock at top right (see also below left).

Sailing ships in Salthouse Dock with Wapping Dock warehouses in the background c1860s.

Dukes Dock and warehouses c1915.

In the footsteps of Jesse Hartley...Albert Dock Heritage Trail

Here is a circular trail you can join wherever it is convenient for you. It should take you about twenty minutes to complete, not allowing for any stops. But, you *will* want to stop! For there are shops you will want to browse in, refreshment places dotted around the quaysides and a number of top class attractions for you to visit.

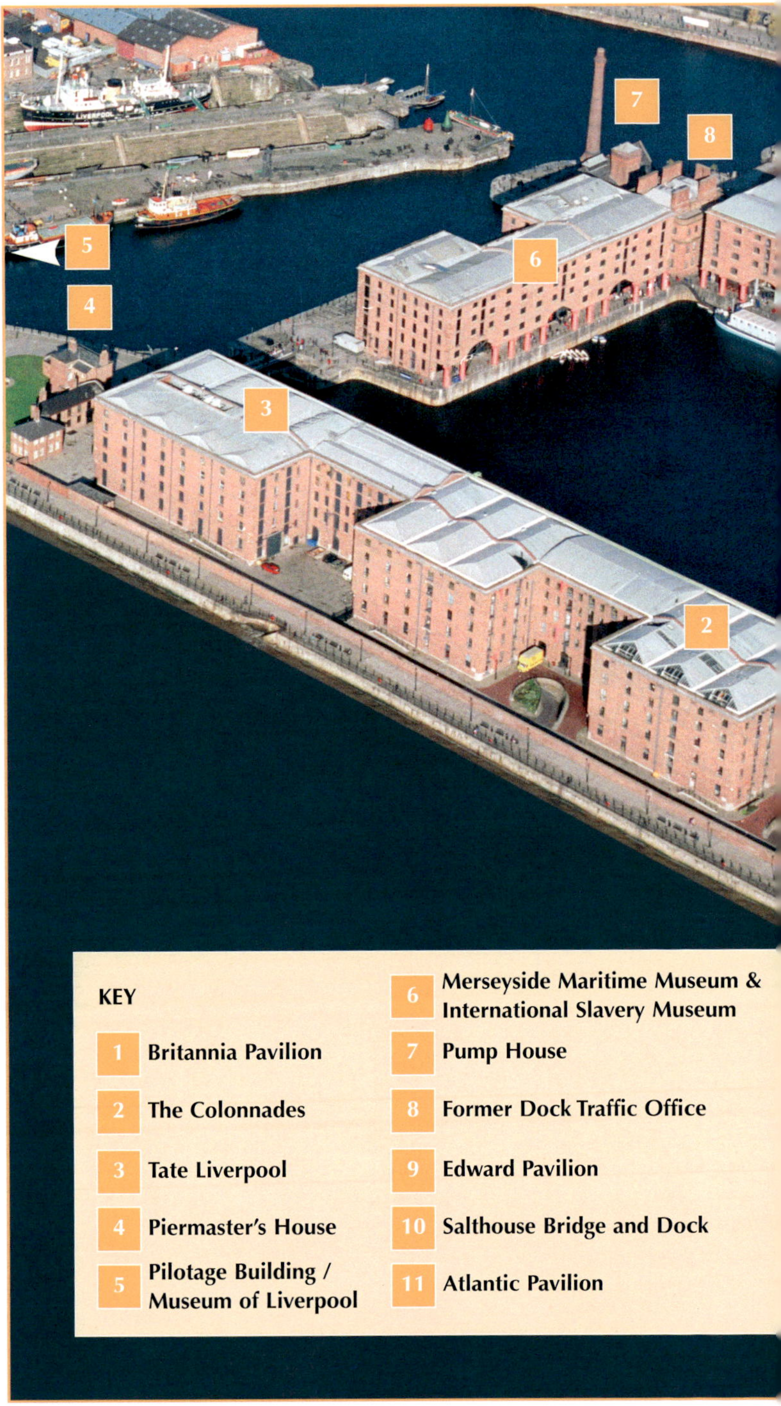
7
8
5
6
4
3
2
KEY
1 Britannia Pavilion
2 The Colonnades
3 Tate Liverpool
4 Piermaster's House
5 Pilotage Building / Museum of Liverpool
6 Merseyside Maritime Museum & International Slavery Museum
7 Pump House
8 Former Dock Traffic Office
9 Edward Pavilion
10 Salthouse Bridge and Dock
11 Atlantic Pavilion

9
10
11
1

map ref 1

Britannia Pavilion

Beside the entrance is a large red hydraulic cylinder which was used to hoist goods up and down the walls onto the various floors. On the walls of the courtyard entrance are many hoists, pulleys, lifts and cranes. To the left of the entrance, in the vaults is The Beatles Story museum, a 'must' for anyone on a Beatles 'pilgrimage' to the city.

Turn left as you enter, exit onto the quayside and turn left. As you walk towards the Colonnades warehouses, stop at the corner for a terrific view of the dock with the Pier Head in the background. Here you will also find one of Albert's curiosities – three massive granite columns, the only ones in the entire dock.

map ref 2

The Colonnades

Vessels would berth along the quaysides and, using ships' tackle, unload onto the covered quayside. There, cargoes would be checked and processed. They would then be distributed within the warehouses by means of hydraulic cranes and hoists. This method was not only time-saving but prevented undue damage to goods in transit and reduced loss by theft. The ground floor has a vast colonnade of cast-iron Doric columns facing into the Dock. At intervals the row of columns is broken by large elliptical arches so that cranes could swing over the quayside. The upper floors are now occupied as offices and apartments. Below, in the vaults, is the car park serving the apartments.

Towards the end of the Colonnades you will come to...

map ref 3

Tate Liverpool

This section was originally part of the warehousing of the West quayside of the Dock. Building was completed in 1847 and it was used for storage of cargoes such as sugar, tea and silk from the Far East, West Indies and India. It now houses the National Collection of Modern Art in the North of England, opened by The Prince of Wales in May 1988. Definitely worth visiting and, apart from some special exhibitions, it's free. *Take note, apart from Bank Holidays, it's closed on Mondays from September to May.*

The next buildings are 'Mermaid House' the Cooperage, Dock Master's office, and the Piermaster's House.

map ref 4

Piermaster's House

The large three-storey brick building facing east was the Pier Master's house. Pier masters had to live near their place of work so that they were available at all times. The Dock Master was in charge of the day-to-day running of the Dock and for this reason his house overlooked the main entrance. The house has been restored to what it would have looked like in 1900 and admission is free. The grassed area was once the site of three other houses for dock officials including the warehouse manager. They were destroyed in World War II air raids. An air raid shelter once stood against the quayside opposite here. Note also the policeman's lodge. At the river entrance gate stand three octagonal, granite dock gateman's huts, built in 1844. They were supplied with gas heating and lighting and their doors face inland for protection against the weather. Albert Dock was only opened at high tide to allow large vessels to enter, whereas the half-tide basin stayed open to the river for much longer to allow for later arrivals. Note the wealth of cast-iron fittings, including gas lamp posts, gate winches and bollards at the entrance.

Cross over the bridge at river entrance to...

map ref 5

The Pilotage Building

This was built in 1883 as the headquarters of the Liverpool Pilotage Service. Pilots guided ships from as far away as Anglesey through the approach channels between sandbanks and into the city's docks. The building is now part of Merseyside Maritime Museum. To the right are the two Canning Graving Docks, constructed between around 1765 and 1768 as 'dry docks' for the repair of wooden sailing ships. One is taken up with the large black and white pilot boat, *Edmund Gardner* which served the port from 1953 to 1981. The other houses the *De Wadden* schooner, built in Holland in 1917 and, after a long career, restored here. Fittingly, she was the last commercial sailing ship to trade to the Mersey.

The Pilotage Building with the Museum of Liverpool in the background.

Return over the river entrance bridge and turn left across the restored Hartley Bridge. On the left is the Canning Half-Tide Dock where two other vessels in the museum's collection, the River Weaver packet ship Wincham and the tug Brocklebank, are usually berthed. To the right is...

map ref 6

Merseyside Maritime Museum & International Slavery Museum

This warehouse was turned into a cold store in 1899. Meat, fish and other perishables were stored and ice supplied to the fishing fleet at Canning Dock. Near the entrance is a large anchor and an ice chute which looks like a spiral staircase. The anchor comes from the famous training ship HMS *Conway* which was anchored in the Mersey until the Second World War. The chute was used to distribute ice through the building and to vehicles outside the warehouse. This (free) museum is well worth a visit; allow at least one hour. Also visit the 4th floor Maritime Dining Rooms for great views of Albert Dock and the Pier Head, and it is the only place where you can still see Jesse Hartley's amazing stressed skin roof. *To the left is...*

Below, left, the museum and its Canning Half-Tide Dock quayside and, below right, the tug 'Brocklebank' moored at the museum's Albert Dock quayside.

map ref 7

The Pump House

The Pump House was built in 1878 to provide water when the Dock was fitted with new hydraulic hoists – 'jiggers' – to improve cargo handling. The Pump House contained coal-fired boilers and a steam engine to pump water to a high pressure. It was later closed and used as a ships' chandlers' store; now it is a pub and restaurant. Behind is the Rennie suspension footbridge over the half-tide dock, built in 1846 for quick access to the Canning graving docks.

Just beyond the Maritime Museum is...

map ref 8

Former Dock Traffic Office

This beautiful building was designed by Philip Hardwick in 1846 with the top storey added by Jesse Hartley in 1848 to provide accommodation for the Chief Clerk. It was built in the form of a classical Greek temple with a cast iron Tuscan portico and pediment. Like a lodge at the entrance to a great country estate, it was designed to impress. It was the main administration office for the Dock and controlled the storage and movement of goods. Hardwick, who designed the St Katharine's Dock warehouses, adjacent to Tower Bridge, London, collaborated with Hartley on various aspects of Albert. Now part of the Centre for the Study of International Slavery.

Cut through the passage between the Dock Traffic Office and Edward Pavilion and turn left onto the quayside.

map ref 8

Edward Pavilion

Hardwick also designed a very elaborate four-sided clock tower for the roof of Edward Pavilion. In itself it was quite an elegant structure but some people argue that it looked out of place on Edward's roof (see page 28). It was dismantled around 1960.

Continue along Edward Pavilion quayside and walk over the Salthouse Bridge linking Edward and Atlantic Pavilions.

map ref 9

Salthouse Bridge and Dock

Originally called the 'Strand Bridge', this replaced a swing bridge which allowed empty ships to pass through to Salthouse Dock. Dating from 1753, this was the second dock to be built in Liverpool. The first, the 'Old Dock', was opened in 1715 but soon proved to be too small. From here you have a panoramic view of the warehouse stacks which Sir James Picton described as "simply a hideous pile of naked brickwork". Note that the brickwork is curved around the corner of the building to deflect blows from the spars of passing ships. On the walls facing the road you will see 'blocked in' windows. At the time the warehouses were built there was a heavy excise duty on glass so its use was kept to a minimum. But knowing that they might be required in the future, windows were provided for by Hartley but not actually installed. Similarly, 'blind' hoistwells were provided to help future-proof the building. One of Hitler's bombs caused considerable damage to this corner of Atlantic Pavilion but you would be hard-pressed to see the repairs which were carried out between 1986 and 1988.

Atlantic Pavilion, pictured in 1984 prior to renovati and showing bricked-up windows and hoist wells.

After the bridge, turn right onto the quayside of...

map ref 10

Atlantic Pavilion

During the opening of the Dock by Prince Albert a massive lunch was served on the first floor. Long tables made from planks laid across tallow casks, seating fashioned from sacks of corn in red cloth and draperies in pink, white and blue set the scene for the meal eaten in such an unusual banqueting hall.

The quayside continues round to Britannia Pavilion, completing the tour.

Outside Atlanti Pavilion can b found one of th original Liverpoc 'Special' Postin Boxes, cast in 186 and installed o this site by Roya Mail in 1987.

'Zebu' moored outside Edward Pavilion with the Merseyside Maritime Museum in the background.

What can I see from here?

The Heritage Trail set out on pages 98-104 explains what you are looking at as you walk around the quaysides of Albert Dock. These two pages explain what you can see from the perimeter of the Dock.

N.B. The 'big wheel' is not a permanent fixture.

Mersey Tunnel Ventilation Station Woodside

Twelve Quays Irish Sea Ferry Terminal

Wallasey and New Brighton →

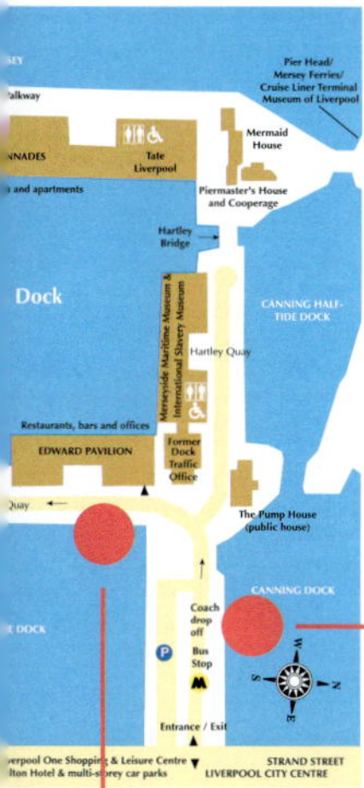

Canning Dock

Museum of Liverpool

Pier Head: Royal Liver / Cunard & Port of Liverpool Buildings

Mann Island Development

One Park West Apartments

Liverpool One

Merseyside Police HQ

Anglican Cathedral

Salthouse Dock (opened 1753)

Wapping Dock Apartments

Royal Quay Apartments

Piermaster's House, 1969. The author pictured at a 'model shoot'; at that time it was considered trendy to use gritty dockland locations. © Photos: Tony Proudlove.

Ron Jones has spent virtually all of his life living and working on Merseyside. As a young boy he enjoyed trips on the Liverpool Overhead Railway, dubbed *The Dockers' Umbrella*, which followed the line of then-busy docks from Gladstone in the north to Herculaneum in the south including, of course, Albert Dock. In the late 60s, as a keen amateur photographer, he took photographs of the derelict Dock and continues to photograph the Dock to this day. Indeed, he claims to have taken more photographs of Albert Dock than any other person, living or dead! Following his appointment as Merseyside County Council's Head of Tourism Development in the mid-1970s, he contributed to the development of the embryonic Merseyside Maritime Museum as well as the general promotion of the re-born Albert Dock. He also acted in a consultancy capacity to the Albert Dock Company for many years.

Since 1988 Ron has run his own marketing communications and publishing company, Ron Jones Associates, which incorporates the Merseyside Photo Library and Liverpool History Press. He is also the author of *The Beatles' Liverpool*, a best-selling guide to Beatle sights in and around Liverpool and a number of other local history books, details of which can be found at – **www.liverpoolhistorypress.co.uk**